ucap,ustx HX 40.S28 1963

Rise of modern communism:

W9-BBO-907

DISCARD

BERKSHIRE STUDIES
IN EUROPEAN HISTORY

Berkshire Studies in European History
Under the editorship of Keith Eubank

*Under the editorship of Richard A. Newhall and Sidney R. Packard

The Rise of
Modern Communism

Starving Russian peasants, early twentieth century. *(Brown Brothers)*

The Rise of Modern Communism

A Brief History of Twentieth-century Communism

REVISED EDITION

. . .

Massimo Salvadori

Smith College

HOLT, RINEHART and WINSTON
New York Chicago San Francisco Toronto London

Copyright 1952, © 1963 by Holt, Rinehart and Winston, Inc.
All rights reserved
Library of Congress Catalog Card Number: 63-22212
03-043760-1
Printed in the United States of America

90123   68   9876

Preface

In this brief historical survey, *communism* means the world-wide movement that originated early in the twentieth century as a small faction within the Social Democratic Labor party of Russian Marxists; it received its theoretical formulation from Lenin's interpretation of Marx, and developed, in the Soviet Union, a set of institutions covering all fields of activity. It means Marxism-Leninism, the common foundation of political parties and states described as communist. Communism was ideologically internationalist from its beginning. It first achieved international political significance in 1918–1921 through the acceptance of Marxism-Leninism by large groups of Marxist socialists in many European countries, and by smaller groups elsewhere. Late in 1963 there were eighty-eight communist parties in as many countries, on all continents.

The point of view reflected in this book is the result of the author's long interest in communism, which dates back to the period immediately following World War I, and his ensuing conviction that communism is incompatible with the freedom he values. This conviction in no way lessens his respect for the sincerity of the communists or his awareness of the idealistic goals pursued by them.

A glance at the literature on communism reveals a considerable variety of opinions. The present survey stresses the consistency of communism both in theory and practice. There are differences, of course, between the communists of the 1920s and those of the 1960s, between Soviet and Chinese communists. Today there is a tendency to see mainly the changes and to ignore or minimize what Marxist-Leninists everywhere have in common. Also emphasized here is the paramount role of ideology in twentieth-century communism, and hence the need to be acquainted with the main ideological points. On this, there is usually agreement. What is not easy, however, is to gauge the relative importance of the basic principles of Marxism-Leninism. Differences in the priority attributed to each principle lead to differences of interpretation—among communists as well as among noncommunists.

Emphasis is commonly placed on the movement's leaders, their quarrels and their intrigues. This survey, however, stresses the importance of the movement itself, particularly in the post-Stalin period. When, as is the case today, there are over 40 million organized members and tens of millions of loyal sympathizers, the movement can act on its own impetus. It is only partially affected by dissensions at the top. It takes a real schism, like that between Khrushchevites and Maoists in 1962, for the whole movement to feel the impact of a dispute among leaders.

Communism cannot be discussed without reference to what communists consider their main enemy. Here again, opinions differ widely. Because many Americans did not become fully aware of communism until the 1930s, it was often identified with antifascism. Considerable disbelief confronts the notion that, since its origin, communism has been and still is, first and foremost antidemocratic (as the term is used in English-speaking nations). Among the elements originally differentiating communism from other currents of the European socialist movement was the greater intensity of the hatred for societies born of the British, American, and French revolutions. These are today's Western democratic societies. During the period when socialism was expanding, they were described by Europeans as "liberal" because they were founded on freedom. When Marxist-Leninist communism was born, many of these societies had become liberaldemocratic. Socialists called them "capitalist" in the nineteenth century, and communists call them "imperialist" in the twentieth. It must be remembered that capitalism and imperialism do not have the same meaning for communists as they have in North America, or wherever free institutions prevail. Lenin's hatred of Russian liberals was greater than his hatred of czarist autocracy. Inherited by today's communists, this hatred is now turned obsessively toward the United States. One of the reasons that led China to attack India in 1962 was the Indians' choice of liberty as the means of solving their problems. To communists, this was worse than the traditional authoritarianism existing in other Asiatic countries. It is enough to glance at the evidence of Latin America to recognize that communists adjust themselves readily to fascist or other rightist dictatorships, but are uncompromising in their opposition to democratic forces.

Terminology presents serious problems. Communism,

democracy, liberalism, capitalism, imperialism are not
the only terms with different meanings. Yesterday's
and today's "isms" have different meanings in different
countries and within the context of different ideologies.
The same political or social phenomenon can, moreover, be described in different terms, depending on
one's sympathies and antipathies, or simply on one's
cultural background. Communism was born in continental Europe and has ever since tended to see situations and problems in terms of those existing during
its formative years—the early decades of this century.
In North America (and, generally, in most English-
speaking countries) situations and problems have been
different from those of continental Europe. Continental
European experiences are not easily translated into
American terms. Here lies one of the difficulties in
trying to provide a correct interpretation of the communist movement. Furthermore, the American interested in communism should keep in mind that the
nations of Latin America and Asia, where communism
is gaining ground, are closer to the experiences of continental Europe than to those of the English-speaking
nations of North America.

The most recent developments within communism,
and in the relationships between communism and other
forces, such as democracy, are mentioned only briefly
in the fifth section of Chapter 3. They belong properly in the field of current events, where abundant
material is readily available.

Smith College   M. S.
1963

Contents

CHAPTER ... 1

The Early Period: Origins and Leninism

European Socialism before 1914

Communism, the world-wide movement ideologically described as Marxism-Leninism, originated in Europe in the years immediately preceding World War I. At that time communism was represented by a small and rather insignificant extremist group within the European socialist movement. The consistency of the Marxist-Leninist doctrine and practice has been remarkable: the main ideological and institutional features either existed when the group was first formed or have been derived from the early characteristic features.

Because of this consistency, and because "all things depend on their origin" (in the words of the Czech philosopher-educator Comenius), it is necessary to go back briefly to the nineteenth century. Of particular importance is the relationship (as seen by the socialists themselves and later by the communists) between socialism and the movement known to Europeans as liberalism, from which it sprang. The socialists both opposed and tried to fulfill the liberal movement. By taking this relationship into account, it is possible to gain a clearer understanding of the communists' position: their goals, their reasoning, and especially their passions.

The nineteenth-century historical scheme accepted by most influential socialists was relatively simple. Traditional absolutism, aristocratic and feudal, was overthrown (as in France) or threatened (as in Russia) by middle-class liberalism, which stressed representative parliamentary institutions and free enterprise (or capitalism). To gain their human rights, workers had to replace liberalism with socialism. (The human rights claimed by the workers were identical to those advocated by the middle-classes, except for the right to individual ownership of property). This scheme of course applied more to continental Europe than to English-speaking nations. Communists apply it to mankind as a whole. It needs to be known because the historical scheme plays an important role in communist thinking.

European liberalism was always a minority movement, but, in or out of power, it remained one of the dominant forces in much of Europe during most of the nineteenth century and the beginning of the twentieth. Progress, though with ups and downs, was considerable. There was, however, increasing dissatisfaction among large sections of European peoples mainly because of two factors. One was the instability of capitalistic economies and the ensuing personal insecurity, which caused much suffering. The other was the liberalization of political institutions, which enabled citizens to express their discontent in larger measure than had ever been possible before. Europeans were considerably less poor around 1900 than they had been a century earlier, but more conscious of their poverty. There was—according to the liberals— less injustice; but there was undoubtedly greater awareness of whatever injustice remained. From consciousness of poverty and awareness of injustice stemmed the social problem, which played an increasingly dominant role during the three decades preceding World War I. In its simplest terms, the social problem derived from the demand of large sections of the population for economic security and a decent standard of living.

To the tensions created internally by the social problem were added the tensions caused by colonialism and imperialism. Through their greater wealth, European states had become more powerful. Freedom of movement had favored the uncontrolled dispersion of tens of millions of Europeans throughout the world. The presence of European travelers, businessmen, and missionaries disrupted civilized and tribal societies in Asia, Africa, Australasia. Half a dozen European states increased their colonial holdings or created new colonial empires, with little effort.

In Europe, around 1900, large sections of the intelligentsia—more and more the dynamic element in all nations—were turning against liberalism. It was rejected *in toto* by the many who were still loyal to the values and institutions of traditional authoritarianism and also by the growing number of racists and extreme nationalists. Among those who shared the liberals' aspiration towards emancipation, accepting some of the fundamental principles of liberalism but rejecting others, the socialists formed the largest group.

The early socialists were French and British. They became vocal in the 1820s when they shared the liberals' hatred for traditional absolutism. They maintained, however, that the evils accompanying the growth of liberalism could be corrected only by curbing individualism and by making society responsible for the triumph of justice. Instead of capitalism they advocated collectivism, varying from public ownership of some basic industries to the socialization of all economic activities. Instead of free movement within a population differentiated economically, politically, and culturally, they advocated the elimination of differentiation. European liberals had aimed at emasculating the state; influential socialist groups, although often talking of the ultimate elimination of the state, were led to strengthen its authority in order to curb the differences that develop within a free society. With a few important exceptions socialists advocated internationalism and liberals generally favored nationalism.

From the beginning, there was a variety of schools of thought in socialism. However, the convictions that made a socialist in Europe in the nineteenth century can be easily summarized: equality was the greatest good; justice was achieved through equality; the community, not the individual, had priority; cooperation should be the norm of human behavior; capitalism was the source of all evil and its antithesis, collectivism, the source of all good. For the sake of comparison: for the European liberal, liberty was the greatest good; justice was the classical *suum cuique tribuere*; equality was moral and legal; individual freedom required the weakening of power exercised by the state; competition was the main source of progress; capitalism increased prosperity more than any other economic system, and collectivism meant the re-establishment of political despotism. Moreover, liberals wanted the citizens to act through constitutional forms and gave constitutions priority over the will of majorities and minorities. Socialists, on the other hand, maintained that no limit should be set on the will of the majority, that constitutionalism (disparagingly described as "formal democracy") was an instrument subordinating the majority to the will of the property-owning minority.

The socialist movement had had its forerunners in the Frenchman F. N. Babeuf (1760-1797), the Italian F. M. Buonarroti (1761-1837), and in a small wing of French Jacobins. After the end of the Napoleonic wars, it developed—slowly at first—against a background of abrupt changes, of an increasingly vivid consciousness of the many existing evils, of the pressure of growing masses of people clamoring for the intervention of society (that is, the government) to bring greater justice and happiness to all. During the 1830s and 1840s, the terms socialism and communism acquired a certain popularity in the industrialized countries of western Europe. Little distinction was made between them during the period when the early socialist groups—usually consisting of a few hundred members, at most—were organized in France, Great Britain, and, later, Germany.

The first phase of the socialist movement came to be known as the phase of Utopian socialism. The derisive term "Utopian" was used to indicate what appeared to later socialists to be the impracticability of the schemes for social reform put forth by the Frenchman Saint-Simon (1760–1825), the Englishman Owen (1771–1858), and others. This phase is usually considered to end with the defeat that troops of the French Republic inflicted on the 1871 revolutionary Commune in Paris. Organized in March 1871 by neo-Jacobins and a variety of socialist groups, the Commune was idealized by the succeeding socialist generation. It became the symbol of what socialism should be politically—a system (as Lenin stated) without police, bureaucracy, or army. The Russian Soviet which gave its name to the Soviet Union, was originally intended to be patterned on the Paris Commune.

By 1871 socialism had made comparatively little headway. However, there had been two developments that were important for the future: the publication of Marx and Engel's *Communist Manifesto* and the influence of Marxists in the Workingmen's Association, better known as the First International.

In France, in 1847, out of a small semiclandestine socialist organization called the Federation of the Just (whose slogan was "Proletarians of all lands unite!") had been formed the Communist League. The League never had any influence and fizzled out in 1852, but its name came down to posterity because a young German then living in Paris, Karl Marx (1818-1883), wrote a pamphlet for it, which was printed in January 1848. He was aided in the drafting of the pamphlet by his friend Friedrich Engels (1820-1895). With the success of the Marxist version of socialism later in the century, the *Communist Manifesto,* which had passed unnoticed when it first appeared, acquired ever greater diffusion. Today it is one of the most widely read political documents.

Like Comte, Hegel, and Spencer, Marx was convinced that he knew the truth about the universe, life, and the whole human condition. (Of course, his truth was incompatible with theirs and just as hypothetical.) He devoted his life to creating a system of ideas that would explain everything, and into which everything would fit. Marx was original in the synthesis he formulated, not in its component elements. These he derived from the French materialist *philosophes* of the eighteenth century, from the Ger-

man philosophers Hegel and Feuerbach, from the
theory of the class struggle as stated by the French
socialists Blanc and Proudhon, from economic principles as enunciated by French socialists, by Ricardo,
Sismondi, and Thompson, particularly those principles concerning value and the tendencies (laws, as
they were called by economists) supposedly inherent
in free enterprise or capitalist economies.

As the result of the initiative of French socialists
in cooperation with British labor leaders, a Workingmen's Association (The First International) had been
established between 1864 and 1867. It was an attempt
to bring together the socialist groups that had by then
been organized in a number of European countries.
These groups differed widely. Some received their
inspiration from the early Utopian socialists; others
from Marx and Engels, who prided themselves on
what they called a "scientific" approach to the study
of man; others from two anarchistically inclined socialists, Proudhon and the Russian Bakunin (1814-1876);
still others from the Italian mystic nationalist Mazzini
(1805-1872) and the German socialist nationalist Lassalle (1825-1864). In Great Britain, France, and Germany there were socialist groups of Christian inspiration. Among Russian exiles in western Europe, a few
heeded the humanitarian socialist Herzen (1812-1870).
Only a few of the socialist groups joined the International. Its most influential leaders were Marx,
Bakunin, and Mazzini. Mazzini soon quarrelled with
Marx and left the International. A bitter conflict
between Bakunin and Marx came to a head in 1872,
and the International lingered on until formally dis-
solved in 1876. Through its participation in the
International, the Marxist group acquired political
significance in the socialist movement.

During the last quarter of the nineteenth century

more lasting attempts were made to organize European socialist groups on a national basis. The attempts were facilitated by the converging of two movements. Large sections of the working people, particularly the skilled industrial workers, were becoming more politically conscious. At the same time, there was increasing awareness of the social problem among some of the intelligentsia. More and more workers were forming associations of all kinds, discussing problems, trying to formulate policies. More and more intellectuals not only became concerned with the problems facing the working people, but also identified themselves with the working classes. Intellectuals often took the initiative in creating cultural centers for promoting the education of workers. It was mainly socialist intellectuals who were instrumental in establishing socialist parties. The leadership of the fast-growing socialist movement at the end of the nineteenth century was prevalently in the hands of intellectuals. (The same is true of the twentieth-century socialist and communist movements.)

In Great Britain were organized the Fabian Society (1883), which advocated collectivism through peaceful and gradual evolution; the Social Democratic Federation (1884), led by the Marxist H. M. Hyndman (1842–1921); the Independent Labor party (1893), linked to the labor organizations. In France the failure of the Commune left a clear field to the Marxists. J. Guesde (1845-1922) and P. Lafargue (1842-1911, a son-in-law of Marx) were among the founders in 1879 of the French Workers' party, transformed into the Socialist party in 1905. In Germany in 1875, followers of Lassalle and Marx united in creating the German Social Democratic party. The main leaders were W. Liebknecht (1826-1900) and A. Bebel (1840-1913). Repressive antisocialist measures introduced by

Bismarck were lifted by William II, and the Social Democratic party made rapid gains. Socialist parties were organized by Marxists in the Austrian Empire, in Italy, Switzerland, and in the democracies of Scandinavia and the Low Countries. In Spain, socialism was represented chiefly by a large and loose organization of anarchosyndicalists, whose main prophet was Bakunin; there was also a smaller Marxist party.

In Russia, in the wake of the ferment of the 1860s and 1870s among sectors of the intelligentsia, and inspired partly by Herzen and partly by P. L. Lavrov (1823-1900), small groups were formed by intellectual socialists, the *narodniki* or populists, whose main aim was propaganda and agitation among the peasantry. They were known as agrarian socialists. In view of their limited success, a few decided in the late 1870s to heed Bakunin and have recourse to violence in the form of individual acts of terrorism. The murder of Alexander II in 1881 by a socialist terrorist led to stringent repressive measures under his successor Alexander III. A socialist Marxist group was organized among Russian exiles in 1883; among its influential members were G. V. Plekhanov (1851-1918), P. B. Axelrod (1850-1928), and V. I. Zasulich (1851-1919). After the death of Alexander III (1894), a less repressive attitude on the part of the authorities facilitated the formation of other socialist groups, among them, in 1895, the League of Struggle for the Liberation of the Working Class. In 1898 a clandestine meeting in Minsk of a few representatives of the league and two other small groups led to the formation of the Russian Social Democratic Labor party (RSDLP), whose membership from then on was composed exclusively of Marxist socialists.

By 1914 socialism was an important element in

the political life of many European nations. However, there was no unified socialist movement despite
the existence, since 1889, of a Second Socialist International. There were several major as well as minor
socialist currents. The largest was composed of those
following the teachings of Marx, whose well-integrated
theory appealed to the middle-class intellectuals and
to the self-educated workers active in the socialist
movement. A second current was formed by syndicalists and anarchosyndicalists who had evolved programs based on various interpretations of the doctrines
of, mainly, Proudhon and Bakunin, and later of G.
Sorel (1847-1922). They wanted to abolish immediately both capitalism and the state. A third current,
agrarian socialism, had developed, particularly in
Russia, where it was organized into the Socialist Revolutionary party that was established clandestinely in
1902. During the early years of the twentieth century
it was the largest and most influential revolutionary
movement in Russia. Agrarian socialism was economically cooperativistic and politically democratic.
It had made its appearance also in the Danubian
and Balkan countries. A fourth current was the evo-
lutionary and democratic socialism represented chiefly
by British Fabianism, a highly respected although
relatively small group.

In Germany, academic economists had formulated
the so-called socialism of the chair, which had found
practical application in Bismarck's state socialism. In
Great Britain and on the Continent Christian socialist
groups had made progress. In most of Europe the
politically influential labor movement was considered
socialist, although its immediate objective was not
the overthrow of capitalism but the improvement of
the conditions of the wage earner within capitalist
economies. Socialism in its various aspects had ap-

peared in the United States, but was making little
headway against the powerful and expanding current
of democratic capitalism. Greater progress was being
made in some of the overseas English-speaking nations
of the British Commonwealth and in a few Asian
countries.

Since the 1870s the history of socialism concerns
not only its growth and diffusion, first in Europe, then
throughout most of the world, but also the competition between various currents and the elimination of
most of them to the advantage of the existing socialist
and communist parties.

At the beginning of this century Marxian socialism
formed the largest and most influential current of
the socialist movement in continental Europe. The
main tenets of Marxism, as understood by the bulk
of its European followers, formed a cohesive ideological system explaining everything and providing a
guide for action. Marxism was often described as
dialectical materialism. Its philosophical postulates
concerned the universe and the nature of man: reality
was identified with Matter; the dialectical principle
was the law of Matter; man was considered as being
exclusively the product of the social environment,
determined by the mode of production; the class
struggle was the expression of the dialectical principle in human societies (classes were the result of
man's relationship to the mode of production); by
understanding the laws of the social process correctly,
man could accelerate it. In Marxian economics, all
value derived from labor; the essential feature of
capitalism (then the dominant mode of production
in Europe) was the appropriation, by parasitic owners
of the means of production, of value legitimately belonging to the producers—the proletariat. The fundamental laws of capitalism were the growing concen-

tration of wealth in fewer hands, the growing intensity of conflicts among property owners, and the growing poverty of the wage earners. Collective ownership
would eliminate exploitation and would lead to communism, an affluent society in which each would
produce according to his abilities and receive according
to his needs. In Marxian politics, the revolutionary
conquest of the state by the proletariat would replace
the dictatorship of the middle class (parliamentarianism or bourgeois democracy) with the dictatorship
of the proletariat; the conquest of the state would
usher in the replacement of capitalism with collectivism. With collectivism finally established, the state
would disappear. Two more points important for all
Marxists were the assumption that the class, not the
individual, acts, thinks, and wills; and that the transition from capitalism to collectivism is inevitable.
Marxists derided so-called Utopian socialists, but
shared with them the vision of total happiness to be
derived from the abolition of private ownership of
property.

Serious differences existed among Marxist socialists.
On the question of the conquest of the state, some
advocated violent revolutionary methods and others
the use of parliamentary procedures. On the timing
of the revolution, some advocated immediacy, others
maintained that it was necessary to postpone the proletarian revolution and to concentrate instead on a
reformist democratic program. On the extent of
collectivism, some Marxists wanted the socialization
of all economic activities, others of only some activities.
On the relationship between socialist organizations
and the proletariat, and on the nature of socialist
organizations, views again differed.

Because of these differences, pre–1914 Marxian socialism, still largely confined to Europe, was far from

forming a homogeneous bloc. A right wing, whose chief spokesman was the French intellectual J. Jaurés (1852–1914), urged collaboration with progressive nonsocialist movements (in the specific case of France, the Radicals). Right-wing socialists maintained that the workers could improve their lot within the framework of the existing societies, and that the growth of governmental intervention in the economic field would lead to gradual transition from capitalism to socialism. A revolutionary left wing was convinced that the capitalist societies would "founder in a series of ever-increasing economic crises. The end would be the upheaval of the proletariat which was not interested in private property . . . and would organize a collectivist society instead of the existing individualistic one." [1] Among the spokesmen for the left wing were the German R. Luxemburg (1870–1919) and the Russian V. I. Ulyanov (or Lenin, 1870–1924). Between right wing and left wing was the large Marxist center, whose main intellectual representatives were the German K. Kautsky (1854–1938) and the Russian G. V. Plekhanov. The center accepted the use of democratic procedure for the conquest of political power but opposed collaboration with nonsocialist movements and parties. The Marxist center controlled most of the continental socialist parties, by 1914 an important element in European states, in which freedom of expression and of organization were a reality.

Lenin and the Bolsheviki

Communism as we know it today owes many of its basic characteristics to one of its leaders and founders,

[1] F. Borkenau, *World Communism*, New York: W. W. Norton & Company, Inc., 1939, p. 20.

whose will became law in one of the largest nations of the world. Vladimir Ilyich Ulyanov, universally known today as Lenin, was born in Simbirsk, a small town on the Volga about 400 miles east of Moscow. Lenin was the son of a competent official in the ministry of education, descended from a family of presumably mixed Slavic and Tartar origin which had been rewarded by the Czarist government with a minor title of nobility. The deciding crisis of Lenin's life came at an early age, in 1887. This was the hanging of his beloved elder brother Alexander who had become implicated in the activities of the terroristic group "Will of the People" (from which the Socialist Revolutionary party afterwards grew). Admitted at the faculty of law of the University of Kazan, Lenin was expelled for having participated in a students' demonstration against the dean. He was permitted to take his examinations at the University of St. Petersburg (later Petrograd, now Leningrad) and graduated in 1891. At the age of eighteen he began to read Marx's works. He practiced law for a short time in Samara, where he founded a small clandestine Marxist group. In 1895 he joined a larger group in St. Petersburg, where he met his future wife and faithful collaborator, N. K. Krupskaya (1869–1939). He went abroad for a short while and exchanged views with leading Russian Marxist exiles. Back in Russia, he was arrested together with L. Martov (J. O. Tsederbaum, 1873–1923) and sent to Siberia. Released early in 1900, he left Russia and joined Russian exiles of Marxian persuasion, members of the RSDLP. Their main center of activities was then Geneva. A man of iron will, great intellectual capacity, and absolute personal integrity, Lenin lived exclusively for the cause in which he believed. When he could not be active as an organizer, he thought and wrote.

During thirty-five years of intense intellectual and political activity, Lenin devoted himself to the interpretation and clarification of points made by Marx and Engels, particularly the elements of Marxian doctrine that were directly concerned with action. He placed greater emphasis than Marx or Engels on the role of violence as an indispensable means to achieve a socialist society. He advocated mass violence but rejected the individual terrorism of Socialist Revolutionaries, anarchists, and anarchosyndicalists. Lenin insisted forcefully on the need to create homogeneous groups of disciplined professional revolutionaries among whom no factionalism or dissent was to be tolerated. As he saw it, the masses were not going to lead, although most other branches of the socialist movement hoped they would. In Lenin's view the masses had to be led. Again more forcefully than Marx, Lenin stressed the role of the state in the achievement of socialism. He rejected parliamentary procedure and the liberal theory of the division of power.

Like other great leaders in history, Lenin combined intellectual rigidity with flexibility in action. Compromises dictated by circumstances did not affect the dogmatism of his ideological scheme. More doctrinaire than most other socialists, he was also more "practical." In this respect, communists have ever since tried to live up to Lenin's example. He saw his political party as an *élite* leading the proletariat. Starting from the *élite* concept of the party, ideological as well as practical considerations led him to create the one-party system, today the essential element of rightist as well as leftist dictatorships. The one-party system was Lenin's greatest contribution to modern political practice.

Relations with liberals were a fundamental problem for Russian socialists. Many inclined to think that socialists (that is, the working classes) should cooperate with liberals (that is, the middle classes) in the overthrow of the czarist regime. In Lenin's mind, liberalism, not czarism, was the main enemy. He hated democratic socialists because intellectually and politically they were close to European liberalism.

Educated in the antinominalistic philosophy that Marx and Engels had inherited from Hegel, Lenin was concerned exclusively with groups, not with individuals. What mattered was the proletariat, not the proletarians; the *bourgeoisie,* not the bourgeois. This disregard for the individual that was characteristic of Lenin and his collaborators, has become one of the fundamental elements in the communist movement—together with the corollary, Whoever belongs to an evil group must of necessity be evil.

Lenin's example—an unflinching devotion to the ideal of socialism (as he called it) and a terrific capacity for work—was an important contribution to the communist movement. For him, as for convinced communists today, everything was subordinated to the "cause." Lenin's function was a catalytic one. He gathered together a few kindred spirits; once a nucleus was formed it attracted others, first Russians and then, after 1917, also non-Russians. Potential communists existed even before 1903. Thanks to the political, economic, and intellectual crises of the first half of the twentieth century, those whom Lenin had helped to find their way joined forces, formed groups (the communist parties), and became a movement. Wherever they achieved power (and by mid-century their power extended over one third of mankind) they used the force of the state to mold in their own image as many of their fellow countrymen as possible, through a monopoly of education and media of communication. Those whom they could not mold they either destroyed ("liquidated") or reduced to impotence by depriving them of the possibility of establishing relations with one another.

The Social Democratic Labor party formed by Russian Marxists was, during most of its nineteen years prior to 1917, largely an underground organization, even when it had representatives in Russia's parliament. Many of its leaders lived in exile in countries of western and central Europe. At the party's second congress in 1903 (in Brussels and later in London), all the delegates agreed to accept the basic Marxian premises, thereby finally differentiating themselves from the Socialist Revolutionaries. Nevertheless, acute dissension arose between a group led by Martov and Axelrod, supported at times by Trotsky (L. D. Bronstein, 1879–1940), and a group led by Lenin, supported at that time by Plekhanov. The dissension centered on the question of party organization: Lenin wanted to sacrifice the belief in the revolutionary capacities of the proletariat to the practical necessity of forming a party of absolutely reliable revolutionaries. Martov and his friends, with a Jeffersonian faith in the masses, saw in a party of professional revolutionaries a continuation of that social differentiation which they wanted to eliminate; they aimed at giving the party a wide popular basis and wanted the members to exercise control over the leadership. The dissension between the two seemed to derive from a difference in degree; but it really derived from a difference in kind.

Lenin's motion to organize the party according to his views was at first defeated by the congress. As the result of minor disagreements, a few of Martov's supporters left; among the remaining participants Lenin happened to have a majority (24 to 20) that approved his motion. From then on Lenin's faction

was known as the Bolsheviki (from *bolshinstvo,* meaning majority); Martov's friends were the Mensheviki
(or minority group). The two factions maintained
separate organizations but remained in the same party
until 1912 when the Bolsheviki formally established
their own party at a meeting in Prague. It was an insignificant group compared to the millions outside Russia
who were active members of the social democratic,
syndicalist, and labor movements of western and central Europe. In Russia it was numerically inferior
to the agrarian Socialist Revolutionaries. The strength
of the Bolsheviki lay mainly in the clarity of their
ideology, the rigidity and high degree of cohesion of
their organization and the flexibility of their policy—
attributes that are among the chief characteristics of
communist organizations today.

The first occasion on which the Bolsheviki could
act according to their revolutionary principles came
during the disorders that accompanied the Russo-
Japanese War of 1904–1905. Since the financial reforms of Alexander III, rapid industrial expansion
had characterized Russian economic life, and St.
Petersburg had become a main industrial city. Violent
spontaneous outbreaks against the czarist administration took place in St. Petersburg and later in other
parts of Russia. Members of and sympathizers with
socialist groups formed revolutionary committees
called soviets, which purported to express the will
of the toiling masses and to be composed of representatives of industrial workers. The most important
soviet, which subsequently determined the manner
in which others were organized, was the St. Petersburg
Soviet. It lasted about three months (October 13–
December 3, 1905) and acted largely as a strike committee. Its first president was a Menshevik sympa-
thizer; after his arrest he was replaced by Trotsky

who, although a member of the Social Democratic party, had tried to keep out of the quarrel between Mensheviki and Bolsheviki. It was at that time that Lenin met his future successor, Joseph Stalin (Josif Vissarionovich Dzhugashvili, 1879–1953).

The 1905 soviets had played only a minor role in the general revolutionary attempts of that period, but they had captured the imagination of revolutionary Russians, and as time passed, more and more importance was attributed to them. The soviets came to represent the spirit and the essence of revolutionarism, and from then on the term became synonymous both with violent socialist revolution and with the political structure created by the revolution. For the Bolsheviki the soviet was the antithesis of the parliament and the embodiment of workers' democracy.

World War I deepened the cleavages in the various socialist groups of Europe, particularly among the Marxists who—in relation to the war—found themselves split into three main factions: those who supported the war effort of their national governments (social patriots); those who opposed the war effort and were for immediate peace at any price (pacifists); and those who were against the war effort of their governments but did not want peace, their aim being the transformation of what they called an imperialistic war into civil wars against democratic and autocratic governments alike (revolutionaries). The largest groups of revolutionaries were the Russian Bolsheviki and the German Spartacus Bund led by R. Luxemburg and K. Liebknecht (1871–1919). Among non-Marxist socialists, syndicalists and anarchosyndicalists sided with the revolutionaries.

The prewar cleavages between right, center, and left had not upset the unity of the Marxist socialist movement to the extent that World War I did. Representatives of the pacifist and revolutionary tendencies met at Zimmerwald, Switzerland, in September 1915 in an attempt to use the influence of the socialist parties to end the war. They organized themselves as a group with Angelica Balabanova as secretary. The revolutionaries had agreed with the pacifists in condemning the "imperialistic" war. But they refused to condemn war as an instrument of social change, and at another meeting in April 1916 at Kienthal, also in Switzerland, attempted to elaborate their own program. The break between the Marxist revolutionary left and the rest of the socialist movement was more than a question of program: it was the manifestation of two opposing temperaments—the tolerant humanitarianism represented by the pacifists and the violent intolerance of the leftist revolutionaries. The war helped to crystallize the difference between moderate socialism, then forming the majority of the European socialist movement, and extreme socialism, from which the communist movement developed.

The Achievement of Communist Control of Russia

The political success of the Bolsheviki (since 1918, communists) in Russia 1917–1921 was as important as Lenin's interpretation of Marx in forging twentieth-century communism. The events of those years have since been an inspiration, an example, and a guide to action for communists everywhere. The institutions established in Russia (since 1922, the Soviet Union) form the pattern for similar institutions wherever communists achieve power. Lenin's political strategy and tactics and his economic policies are those of communists in places as distant as the Antilles and south-east Asia. Only the names vary. The attitude of the

Bolsheviki towards the Allies, czarism, Kadets, anti-Bolshevik and pro-Bolshevik socialists, was the attitude decades later of the communists in South Vietnam and Cuba toward the United States, toward "feudal" traditional forces, toward democrats described as imperialists, and socialists described as lackeys of imperialism if anticommunist (but as proletarian brothers if willing to collaborate with the communists). Reference to Lenin's peasant policies is made by communists wherever the peasantry is an important class. The soviets, the Cheka, the Red army, the Terror, economic "war communism," the NEP were the tools used by the Bolsheviki to achieve and keep power. With other names, they were the tools used thirty years later in the Far East and Eastern Europe.

A brief summary of the main events 1917–1921 helps explain the impact of the Russian revolution on the later development of world communism. At the end of the winter of 1917, war for the Russians had already lasted over two and a half years. Casualties had been appalling: about 2 million dead and wounded in 1916 alone. Economic conditions had deteriorated considerably, especially in the cities. Among the nearly 400,000 industrial wage earners of Petrograd there was acute consciousness of the need for higher wages and food. There was not yet an active antiwar movement, but the desire for peace was widespread. Spontaneous demonstrations and strikes on March 8, International Woman's Day, got out of hand. On March 12, troops that had been ordered to quell the demonstrations joined the strikers. The czarist administration collapsed and on the 15th the czar abdicated.

There were several groups willing to fill the political vacuum left by the sudden disintegration of the czar's authority. The Constitutional Democrats (Kadets) and the Octobrists (moderates satisfied with the limited

constitution granted in October 1905) wanted to reform
Russia along the lines of Western free institutions.
The Kadet party, organized in 1905 through the
fusion of various progressive groups, had had 179
deputies out of 478 in the Duma (chamber of deputies
or parliament) elected in 1906. Its representation had
been cut considerably in the succeeding elections but
it was still considered the mainstay of liberal forces
in Russia. Its most influential leader was P. N. Miliukov (1859–1943). The Octobrist group had as main
spokesman A. J. Guchkov (1862–1936). Miliukov had
organized among members of the Russian parliament
the Progressive Bloc, a coalition of center and right-
of-center groups. Both Kadets and Octobrists were
more influential in the Duma, elected on the basis
of limited and differential suffrage, than among the
people. They derived their support from the majority
of the Russian middle class and from the enlightened
minority of the upper classes—two groups that included only a fraction of the Russian nation.

Among socialists, the most numerous were the
Socialist Revolutionaries. Their socialism was economically more of the cooperativistic than of the collectivist variety; politically they were democrats and
federalists. They rejected both the theory and the
practice of state omnipotence. There was a right-wing
majority led by V. M. Chernov (1876–1952) and a
left-wing minority in which a woman, M. Spiridonova,
exercised considerable influence. According to Chernov, the Socialist Revolutionaries envisaged a long
transition period from capitalism to socialism, during
which social reforms would be introduced within
the frame of a money economy. To the right of the
Socialist Revolutionaries was the small group of
Trudoviki or Laborites. Among their leaders was
a young lawyer and deputy to the Duma, A. Kerensky

(1881–   ), who later joined the Socialist Revolutionary party. The two other socialist groups were the Marxist Mensheviki and Bolsheviki. Among the influential Mensheviki present in Petrograd were N. S. Chkheidze (1864–1926) and I. G. Tseretelli (1882–1959).

In Petrograd, the various groups struggled for power in a multiplicity of committees, clubs, and leagues that had mushroomed overnight. In the streets and squares there were parades, meetings, and demonstrations—and some violence, although remarkably little at first. On March 16, 1917, the leaders of the Progressive Bloc, headed by Prince G. E. Lvov (1861–1925), had formed a provisional government that included Miliukov, Guchkov, and Kerensky. Before this, on March 9, Socialist Revolutionaries and Mensheviki had organized a soviet, which began to function on the 12th. The soviet supposedly represented the will of workers and soldiers. (Peasants joined it in November 1917.) The same dualism of authorities, some loyal to the provisional government and others to the soviets, existed in other Russian cities.

During the months immediately following the March revolution, events in the provinces, which were of greater importance than those in the capital, permanently influenced communist policies toward the peasantry. For the masses of Russian peasants, the abdication of the czar meant that there was no longer a government, that it was now possible to realize the aspiration of most peasants in most countries at most times: to own the land they cultivate. As in France shortly after the meeting of the Estates General in 1789, so in Russia (but not immediately) there was a *jacquerie,* an unorganized and all-powerful revolt of the tillers of the soil. This became an irresistible force at the end of the summer. It is usually difficult to get the peasantry to move; once they start, it is even more difficult to stop them; and where peasants form a large percentage of the population (as in Russia in 1917) they can crush everything under their weight. The peasants began to kill the landlords and to divide the land among themselves; the soldiers (most of whom were peasants) began to kill their officers; the workers in the towns and the miners (most of them only a few years removed from the soil) began to kill their employers. The riots in the capital had led to the czar's abdication. The *jacquerie* destroyed what organization of the Russian state still remained. It created the chaos that was to enable a small but determined minority to establish itself as the new Russian state.

The war against Germany was a complicating factor. Members of the provisional government were for the continuation of the war. The Bolsheviki, following the line set by Lenin at Zimmerwald and at Kienthal, opposed the continuation of the war on the side of the Allies. This attitude seemed to vindicate those who thought that the Bolsheviki were nothing but German agents; they proved, however, to be faithful representatives of the aspirations of the dynamic sections of the masses.

At the time, the Bolsheviki were not numerous. Lenin estimated their numbers at about 240,000 in July 1917, of whom 32,000 were in Petrograd. An American expert on Russian and communist affairs, F. L. Schumann, states that "the army of the faithful numbered only 40,000 in April 1917, and only 115,000 early in 1918." A British expert, E. H. Carr, gives the figure at 23,600 for February 17, 1917. Whatever the exact total, the Bolsheviki in 1917 were numerically a rather insignificant group, drawn from the intellectuals rather than from the workers. When

Nikolai Lenin. (*Brown Brothers*)

rioting in Russia's capital acquired the aspect of a revolt, the Bolsheviki at first were uncertain about the attitude they should adopt. Several leaders apparently played with the idea of collaborating with other anticzarist groups. Lenin arrived in Petrograd at the beginning of April in the sealed railroad coach which, through the intervention of Swiss socialists, the German authorities had put at the disposal of several Russian exiles and which brought them from Switzerland across Germany. Lenin's arrival put an end to the vacillations of the Bolsheviki, who were joined in the summer by Trotsky and about 4,000 of his friends. Trotsky had never until then been a strict Leninist. He had, however, agreed with Lenin that the main enemy was not czarism but the liberal middle classes.[2]

The Bolsheviki wanted nothing in common with the provisional government. "The new government cannot bring peace . . . cannot give the people bread . . . nor full freedom," wrote Lenin. And Trotsky echoed: "The handing over of power to the Liberals . . . will become . . . a source of headlessness of the revolution, enormous chaos, embitterment of the masses, collapse of the front, and in the future, extreme bitterness of the civil war." Avoiding the encumbrances and limitations of parliamentary procedure "the Soviet of Workers', Soldiers' and Peasants' deputies must at once take every practical and feasible step for the realization of socialism."[3] What government by soviets meant was explained by Trotsky: "In the system of Soviet dictatorship not even a secondary place was found for democratic representation" when

[2] I. Deutscher, *The Prophet Armed,* London: Oxford University Press, 1954, pp. 129f.
[3] V. I. Lenin, *Collected Works,* New York: International Publishers Co., Inc., Vol. XX, Book I, p. 159.

the Bolsheviki took over. More important than Bolshevik influence in the soviets was the organization of an armed force in October, the work of Trotsky who headed a Military Revolutionary Committee controlling several thousand enthusiastic proletarians.

Developments in the provisional government, in the Petrograd Soviet, in the few but important industrial cities, in the rural districts where the overwhelming majority of the population lived, and at the front were the main elements in the chaotic situation of Russia after March 15, 1917. In July, Kerensky succeeded Lvov as prime minister, but the organs through which government orders were implemented were already disintegrating. The armed forces of the Soviet, not government troops, prevented general Kornilov from carrying out his own *coup d'état* in September. Through patient, unremitting efforts the Bolsheviki increased their participation in the Petrograd Soviet; a revolutionary attempt in July failed, but through a split in the Socialist Revolutionary party and with the help of the Left Socialist Revolutionaries they achieved control of the Soviet by October 1917. The Bolsheviki became increasingly influential in the soviets, which exercised power in the industrial cities of Russia. When delegates were chosen for the second all-Russian congress of Soviets, the Bolsheviki had a plurality—300 out of some 650. In the rural districts, the *jacquerie* had ended all forms of organized government authority by the end of October. Together with this came the disruption of transportation and economic chaos. On the front, chiefly after the failure of the half-hearted summer offensive against the Germans—undertaken at the Allies' request— entire divisions had disintegrated, and in others officers had been replaced by soldiers' soviets. Russia was a name, no longer a political entity.

On November 7, 1917 (new calendar), the second congress of Soviets met in Petrograd. During the night the military squads organized by Trotsky occupied the key points of the capital. Kerensky fled. Lenin, whose slogan "Peace, Land, Bread" had attracted larger and larger groups of the population, formed a new government composed of commissars. Among them, besides himself and Trotsky, were A. M. Kollontai (1872–1933), A. I. Rykov (1881–1938), and Stalin. The second congress of Soviets, in which the Bolsheviki and their allies, the Left Socialist Revolutionaries, had a majority, enthusiastically acclaimed the leaders of the *coup d'état*. Small anti-Bolshevik insurrections were put down easily. After some bloodshed, the Bolsheviki gained control of Moscow.

Censorship of the press, an essential instrument of despotism, was established on November 17. On December 20 an even more essential instrument came into existence, the secret police—the Cheka, headed by the Pole F. Dzierzynski (1877–1926), one of Lenin's most loyal friends. Early in January the Constituent Assembly met. It originally included 175 Bolsheviki, about 40 fellow-traveling Left Socialist Revolutionaries, 370 other Socialist Revolutionaries, 16 Mensheviki, 17 Kadets, and deputies of other groups. The Kadets had been outlawed and a number of Socialist Revolutionaries arrested. In spite of these intimidations the Assembly voted a motion of no-confidence in the Bolshevik government. The latter reacted with an order to dissolve the Assembly, which was carried out by Trotsky's troops. In March 1918, at the 7th party congress, the official name of the Bolshevik organization was changed to Communist party. The seal was put on the difference between Bolsheviki and all other socialists.

The success of the Bolsheviki was astounding. It

was due to their cohesion, the decisiveness of their leaders, the disintegration of the Russian state, the *jacquerie,* the divisions among their opponents, the pressure of foreign (German) attack, and the will for peace of the Russian nation.

During the first months of the Bolshevik regime little was done to introduce collectivism in the country. Lenin, who knew what to destroy but had only a vague idea of how to organize the collectivist society, considered this a transitional period in which there would be a mixed economy, partly state-managed and partly private. The plan was, apparently, to transform Russia gradually from an agrarian to a modern industrial nation, to extend the sphere of nationalized enterprises in industry and trade, while checking the growth of a new economic middle class by taxation and controls. By the end of May 1918 (new calendar), only 300 concerns and some agricultural estates representing about 4 percent of the tilled land of the country had been nationalized.

The decision to put an end to the first brief "transitional" period and to force the over-all introduction of collectivism was taken as a result of Russia's political disintegration, which grew after the *coup d'état* of October 1917. By the summer of 1918 the communist government held authority over areas inhabited by less than one fourth of the Russian population. It became evident that the limited popular support the Bolsheviki (now communists) had enjoyed was waning, and that only through force could they keep themselves in power. The choice was between terror and failure. Under the guidance of Dzierzynski a reign of terror was established to eliminate all opposition in the areas still controlled by the communist government. Anticommunist revolutionaries (anarchists, Socialist Revolutionaries, and Mensheviki) were liquidated as savagely as the Kadets, the Octobrists, and the members of the former privileged groups. Following requests of Western socialists, a few anti-Bolshevik leaders, particularly among the Mensheviki, were allowed to leave Russia. Millions escaped without passports, leaving everything behind. From the ranks of party members, refugees from regions that no longer recognized the authority of the central government, and remnants of the Russian armies, a Red army was organized by Trotsky. His energy was probably the most important single factor in saving communism at the most crucial period of its development. Tens of thousands of officers of the former czarist forces consented to serve in the Red army and cooperated with the Bolsheviki.

In the economic field, an attempt was made to bring all available resources under the control of the government to strengthen its authority and to supply the Red army. All industrial concerns were now nationalized. The peasants were compelled to surrender the major part of their produce to the government; private ownership of homes was abolished, as was money, which was replaced by a system of coupons.

The struggle to eliminate organized opposition against the communist regime lasted nearly three years, or a little longer if one takes into account events on the periphery of the Russian state. The Ukraine lost its newly-won independence at the end of 1920. The Menshevik regime in Georgia was defeated in February 1921, the pan-Turanian leader Enver Pasha was killed and his followers dispersed in August 1922, and the Far Eastern Republic originally sponsored by the Japanese was reincorporated in the Russian state in November 1922. After the liquidation of the Socialist Revolutionaries (facilitated by their internal divisions), the greatest threat to the communist regime was represented by the "White" armies organized in the arctic north, in the Baltic areas, in the south, in Siberia—and also by the troops of the newly-established Polish republic that attacked Russia in 1920. The description of the happenings of those years belongs properly to the history of Russia. For our purposes, it is enough to mention that jealousies between leaders, excesses that alienated the peasant population, the aggressiveness, determination, and courage of the Red army, and Trotsky's genius and ruthlessness put an end to the "White" opposition after two and a half years of furious and bloody fighting. A limited amount of help had been given by some Allied powers to some of the anticommunist forces: not enough to win, but enough to provide a further rationalization for the intense hatred of the communists towards anything Western. At the peak of their strength, foreign forces numbered about 100,000 men spread from Vladivostock in Siberia to Odessa on the Black Sea, from Arkhangelsk on the Arctic Ocean to Tiflis in Georgia: not a force but a farce.

The end of the civil war found Russia exhausted. In spite of the victory, dissatisfaction, exemplified by the Kronstadt revolt (March 1921) at the cry of "the Soviets without the Communists," was widespread. Terror had all but destroyed the will to opposition among the educated classes; but it was doubtful whether it would have the same effect on the increasingly restive uneducated masses, and whether it would be enough to keep the government in power. To satisfy large sections of the population, both in the rural areas and in the cities, the 10th party congress (March 1921) decided to recognize private trade and small-scale private production, thereby introducing the New Economic Policy (NEP), which represented a return to Lenin's transitional period in the early stages of the regime. Violent disputes arose at once in the Council of Commissars and the Political Bureau of the party between Bukharin (1888–1938), Kamenev, Rykov, Tomsky (1880–1936), Trotsky, Zinoviev (1883–1936), and others over the extent of the concessions to be made to nonsocialist economic forces, with Lenin acting as final arbiter.

The success of the Bolshevik revolution in Russia was of fundamental importance in the later development of the communist movement. If communism had remained confined to the West, it would probably have died out like anarchism, syndicalism, and other extreme movements. In the West the liberal democratic trend was strong enough to eliminate movements it could not absorb. Their success in Russia gave the communists the backing of one of the most powerful states in the world. Moreover, the triumph in Russia strengthened those traits in the communist movement that are closely linked to a culture which has hardly known, and cares less for, the elements that made possible the development of modern free Western societies: respect for the dignity of the individual, moderation, belief in the superiority of government by discussion and of the rule of law, the legitimacy of opposition and dissent. Socialism had been a development of Western civilization: It had derived its strength from a deep humanitarian impulse. It might have been mistaken in the assumption that collectivism produces greater liberty than capitalism, but it was animated by a sincere desire to achieve greater individual liberty through greater equality and more justice. Communism was socialism interpreted by a society characterized to the highest degree by political autocracy and intellectual intolerance. It was unlimited collectivism, to be realized through the integral collectivization not only of the economy but of all forms of human activity.

The Revolutionary Phase
of the Comintern (1919-1923)

At the time of the armistices that put an end to World War I (September-November 1918), conditions seemed to favor the success of revolutionary movements in many parts of Europe. Human suffering had been great. The war had affected practically every family in most countries. The institutions established during the nineteenth century had weakened. Economic losses had been heavy. Four years of deep nervous strain were bound to cause a reaction. Besides the Russian empire, the German, Austro-Hungarian and Ottoman empires had also collapsed. These, together with the Balkan states, overrun by the contending armies, covered two thirds of the European continent. Confusion and chaos reigned over large areas. Elsewhere, there was considerable tension. In Italy, in France, even in the British Isles, many worried about the possibility of violent social revolutions. Here was an ideal situation for small groups to seize the political initiative. The Russian revolution had caused repercussions in every corner of the Continent. It had raised the hopes of the revolutionaries; its excesses had terrified not only conservatives and liberals but also the great majority of socialists.

Immediately after the end of hostilities, in various countries small socialist groups that shared the ideology of the Bolsheviki made definite attempts to follow Lenin's example and to seize power. The attempts failed. In Finland, the revolutionary government set up by Kuusinen (1881–   ), leader of the leftists among the Social Democrats, had been defeated through the combined efforts of anticommunist Finns and German troops. In the former Baltic provinces (which had become the independent republics of Lithuania, Latvia, and Estonia) the presence of Germans and of "White" (antirevolutionary) Russians made the organization of a communist movement impossible. In Poland, the nationalistically-minded Socialist party led by Pilsudski (1867–1935) won over the more extremist Social Democratic party. Rumanians were more interested in wresting Transylvania from Hungary and Bessarabia from Russia than in revolution. In Bulgaria the peasants' Agrarian party led by Stamboliiski (1879–1923), in power since September 1918, was close to the Bolsheviki's bitter foes, the Socialist Revolutionaries. In Hungary, moderate republicans led by M. Karolyi (1875–1955) were able to form a government, and in Austria the powerful left-inclined socialists under Otto Bauer (1881–1938), besides being opposed to the violent tactics used by the communists in Russia and advocated elsewhere by communist sympathizers, were convinced that the time was not ripe for socialism. In Czechoslovakia, under the leadership of T. Masaryk (1850–1937), nationalism and liberalism won out over revolutionary socialism.

It was in Germany that conditions appeared to be most favorable for the development of a situation similar to the one in Russia. What had been for decades the strongest, largest, and best organized Marxist socialist movement in Europe existed there. Majority Socialists and Independent Socialists (respectively, the social patriots and the pacifists hated by Lenin and his friends) had the support of the majority of German industrial workers and of large sections of the middle classes. The more radical socialist groups, the Spartacists and the Shop Stewards,

also had a considerable following, but it proved to be
inadequate. In November 1918, Majority and Independent Socialists had formed a provisional government that easily repressed the sporadic risings organized
by the extremists in December. Through the initiative
of Rosa Luxemburg and Karl Liebknecht, a Communist party (the first in Europe outside Russia) was
formed on December 31, 1918. It organized another
rising for the middle of January 1919. This failed,
and the two leaders were killed. In Berlin, as in
Petrograd, a Workers' and Soldiers' Council (Soviet)
had been organized; but instead of trying to overthrow the provisional government, it (in the words
of Borkenau) "voted itself out of power by a big
majority, deciding to hold the polls for a Constituent
Assembly," loyally respecting the expression of the
popular will. In southern Germany the revolutionary
movement had apparently petered out with the formation of a provisional government in Bavaria under the
pacifist socialist Kurt Eisner (1867–1919), a foe of the
communists.

In France and Italy Marxist parties were large and
well organized; there were smaller syndicalist and
anarchosyndicalist groups. But contrary to Lenin's
expectations, the end of the war did not immediately
bring revolutionary agitation; there was a partial political lull for several months, which was largely due
to exhaustion. There seemed to be more of a revolutionary situation in Spain; here, however, anarchosyndicalists, foes of Marxism, looked suspiciously at
events in Russia. Except for a few intellectuals, British
socialists were staunch democrats and did not entertain
violent revolutionary ideas. Lenin had had many
friends among Dutch, Scandinavian, and Swiss socialists, but at the end of 1918 there were already strong
feelings of revulsion among them against the communists' terrorism in Russia.

It was evident that in western and central Europe the revolution would not take place as easily as had been hoped. The Bolshevik leaders called a conference in Moscow (once again the capital of Russia) in order to launch an international organization through which the revolutionary groups following the line of the Russian communists could help each other. It was maintained that by strengthening the revolutionary groups in the countries of western and central Europe, a general European revolution could follow in the wake of the Russian one. The meeting was not well attended. On March 7, 1919, the Third or Communist International was launched—the Comintern, as it came to be known all over the world. The first secretary was Angelica Balabanova, a pacifist; Gregori Zinoviev, Lenin's long-time friend and collaborator, was appointed president.

Hopes ran high. Zinoviev prophesied that "within a year . . . all Europe would be a Soviet Republic." Great efforts were made to realize the hopes: the four and a half years from March 1919 to October 1923 saw a series of definite attempts on the Comintern's part to achieve a communist dictatorship in several European countries.

The murder of Kurt Eisner in Munich induced the local Independent Socialists to proclaim a Soviet republic on April 7, 1919. Six days later this government was overthrown by the communists under the leadership of Eugene Leviné. A few Russian communists appeared on the scene but were of little help. Unable to organize the defense of the city, attacked by the troops of the predominantly Social Democratic central government, the Bavarian communist regime was ousted by the other socialist groups under the leadership of the poet Ernst Toller. On May 1 the government troops entered Munich, and Leviné was killed.

In Hungary the democratic provisional government

under Karolyi resigned on March 20, 1919, as a protest against excessive Allied demands. With the help of the socialists, the communist Bela Kun (1886–1936) set up a new regime that included, as deputy commissar of commerce, Mathias Rakosi (M. Roth, 1893–   , after the events of 1944–1947 until 1956 the real ruler of Hungary). The new government immediately abolished private property in all means of production and decreed the death penalty for everyone engaging in trade. The Russians, pressed by several "White" offensives, were unable to send any help. Rumanians and "White" Hungarians attacked the new Soviet republic. The massacres ordered by Tibor Szamuely, a firm believer in the most ruthless violence, alienated the masses, particularly in western Hungary. The Austrian socialists were repelled by terrorism and refused to help the Hungarian extremists. The Hungarian Soviet republic collapsed on August 19, 1919, and was replaced by a government of moderate trade-unionists, soon overthrown by reactionary groups. Europeans were shocked at the time by the excesses of Bela Kun's regime, which strengthened anticommunist feeling and magnified the fear on which reactionary movements thrive. For many Europeans, Russia was a distant country, but Hungary lay in the heart of Europe and the Hungarian revolution had seemed a greater threat than the Russian one.

During this period the cleavage between democratically-minded socialists and the communists increased. The tension between the former social patriots and the pacifists prevented the reorganization of the Second International at the two meetings of March 1919 in Berne, and of August in Lucerne. However, there was no doubt that the two wings were closer to each other than to the communist groups. Former antiwar socialists, including, among others, the Independent

Socialists of Germany and the French and Austrian
Socialist parties (the so-called Reconstructionists),
launched a new International (the Second-and-a-half
International) in 1921, supported by the Trade Union
International organized in Amsterdam by Edo Fimmen.

This development was interpreted as an act of hostil-
ity against the communists. Thus, it induced the leaders
of the Comintern to adopt a more intransigent attitude, exemplified in the communication they sent to
the Independent Socialists of Germany. In it they
criticized:

> the idea that the support of the majority of the people
> is necessary for the establishment of the proletarian dic-
> tatorship; [the] rejection of revolutionary terrorism; lack
> of readiness to face civil war; lack of understanding of
> the necessity of wrecking the machinery of the *bourgeois*
> state; [the] petty-*bourgeois* insistence upon the safe-
> guarding of democratic liberties; [the] useless attempts to
> win the lower middle classes; [the] vague talk about
> nationalization, when a clear-cut fight for expropriation
> without compensation would be necessary.

To strengthen the communist movement, the second
world congress of the Third (Communist) International had been held in July 1920. It was attended
by delegates of the Russian Communist party, the
Italian, Norwegian, and Bulgarian Socialist parties,
the Czech Left Socialists, the Communist parties of
Hungary and Austria, both the German Communist
party and the German Independent Socialist party,
among others. It approved a twenty-one-point program that stressed the decision to fight not only the
bourgeoisie but also all reformist, reconstructionist,
centrist, patriot, and antiwar socialists. It required the
development of underground organizations, the sub-

version of the peasantry, the breaking of the Trade
Union International, the obedience of communist
parliamentarian groups to the executive committees
of the various parties, the centralization of authority
in all communist parties and their subordination to
the Comintern, periodical purges, and the exclusion
of all members who did not vote for affiliation with
the Communist International. As long as the Comintern functioned, the twenty-one points guided communist action everywhere.

Attempts were made to bring together the various
Marxist factions, but they failed before the intransigence of both communists and social democrats, who
were deeply divided on the fundamental problems
of human freedom, individual rights, and the use
of violence. When the Second-and-a-half International
of former pacifist socialists tried to bring together
the Third International (the Comintern) and the
Second International finally reorganized by the social
democratic parties, the Belgian socialist Vandervelde
(1866–1938) asked, as the price for the agreement,
that Russia adopt representative institutions, establish
freedom of press and propaganda for the noncommunist socialist groups of Russia, liberate Russian
Socialist Revolutionary leaders, and recognize the
independence of Georgia. These requests were refused by Lenin and Zinoviev (except for the reprieve
of the death sentence for the Socialist Revolutionaries). Thus the projected unification of the many
branches of the socialist movement did not take place,
the field being clearly divided between democrats
(the Second International) and antidemocrats (the
Third International), between socialists whose collec-
tivistic aspirations were checked by the European
liberal tradition, and integral or totalitarian socialists.

Nineteenth-century socialism had been antiliberal

because it wanted more liberalism; it had operated on the basis of two contradictory elements, liberal aspirations and opposition to liberalism, which now were clearly divorced. Democratic socialists came to the conclusion that the desired extension of liberalism was incompatible with the destruction of what liberalism had achieved (democracy); communists denied liberalism *in toto*. The triumph of the Bolsheviki in Russia transformed the socialist movement. Many pre–1917 divisions previously mentioned weakened: on one side there were the democratic socialists, on the other the communists.

Having achieved greater cohesion within the movement, the communist leaders renewed their revolutionary efforts. But now the tide was against them. A few small risings, like the one in Estonia, failed even to arouse popular interest. In Italy there was practically a state of civil war in 1921 and 1922, but the communists made little or no headway. The last serious attempts of the communists during this phase took place in Germany in October 1923, when Brandler, then the leader of the German Communist party, was ordered to prepare for a rising. First he accepted a post in the coalition cabinet of the state of Saxony, with the aim of acquiring control over the police. The rising took place, but the population remained indifferent, and the troops of the central government had no difficulty in suppressing the revolt. Other risings, in Thuringia and Hamburg, also failed. The Communist party was outlawed in Germany but was made legal again a few months later.

Although Europe was, and remained for a considerable time, the main theater of communist activities, attempts were made during this first phase of the Comintern to develop communist organization elsewhere. The United States, before World War I, had

witnessed the expansion of some socialistic movements;
among them the Socialist party, which had increased
its voting strength ninefold between 1900 and 1912,
and the Industrial Workers of the World, basically a
syndicalist organization. The syndicalists, among whom
at the time was W. Z. Foster (1881–1961), later leader
of the American Communist party, emphasized the
use of force and violent revolution, and had decided
to transfer the functions of the state to the workers'
organizations as soon as they could gain power. The
great majority of the socialists accepted, instead, the
free political institutions and the fundamental ideological principles of the American republic. A minority,
although disagreeing with the syndicalists on the position of the state, were convinced that violence was
necessary to bring about a social revolution; these
constituted the so-called left wing, whose members
sympathized warmly with the Russian Bolsheviki.
Factional strife was intense. In 1919, from the left
wing of the Socialist party, arose a Communist party
and a Communist Labor party. They represented a
negligible element in the life of the American nation
for they were based on unassimilated groups, whose
communism was often nothing but an expression of
Slavic nationalism, and on the unstable fringe of the
intelligentsia.

The repression at the end of 1919 was caused partly
by reaction against the excesses of communism in
Europe. It drove the American communists underground. In 1920 an effort was made to unite the
Communist party and the Communist Labor party,
which combined to form the united Communist party.
Under the conditions of freedom and personal security
enjoyed by American citizens, communist leaders
found it impossible to enforce unity among the few
thousand communists then existing in the country,

and by the end of 1921 there were no less than twelve different communist organizations, each group accusing the other of being "petty-bourgeois," an accusation implying attachment to the institutions of liberal democracy and unwillingness to use collective terrorism. The economic crisis of 1921 seemed to provide a favorable juncture for a revolutionary movement. Several warring communist factions joined hands in a new Workers' party. To help in the unification, Moscow sent a representative, who ordered rebellious members to join the Workers' party. Following the directives of the Comintern, the American communists devoted themselves to the formation of a cohesive communist organization and to the development of "fronts" through which a large number of people could be reached.

In China, where political disintegration had increased rapidly after the revolution of 1911, a Communist party had been established in 1921. There was an agreement in 1923 between Sun Yat-sen (1866–1925), leader of the democratic section of the revolutionary movement, and the Soviet rulers. As a result, the Chinese communists, under the guidance of the Soviet representative Borodin, made a definite effort to conquer Sun's party, the Kuomintang, the organization of which was patterned on the Russian Communist party. There was a semblance of democratic control by the members and a reality of domination by a small group. But many feared that success for the revolution at the price of communist leadership would mean that it was a Russian, not a Chinese, revolution. As a result, after the death of Sun Yat-sen, a struggle broke out between the strictly nationalistic wing of the Kuomintang, led by Chiang Kai-shek (1887–   ), and the communists. The outcome was the departure of the Russian agents and, at least for a while, the unification of most of China under nationalist leadership. Pockets of communist activity remained here and there under various leaders, among whom the ablest and most energetic were Mao Tse-tung (1893–   ), son of a central China peasant, and Chu-Teh (1886–   ), of a well-to-do family.

By the end of 1923, with the exception of China, communism outside Russia was definitely on the defensive. Revolutionary activity had not led to the hoped-for results. Agrarianism (in Bulgaria), nationalism (in Poland and Rumania), fascism (in Italy and Hungary), social democracy (in Germany, Austria and Scandinavia), and liberalism (in France, the smaller Western democracies, and the English-speaking nations) had proved to be stronger than communism. Again with the exception of China, in the economically less advanced sections of the world communism had had little or no impact. In India, Indonesia, Japan, the Middle East, and Latin America, there were individual communists, sometimes grouped in numerically insignificant parties, but as yet no communist movement.

The First Struggle for Succession
(1924-1927)

That communism had been based on a number of fallacies was clear by 1923. Industrial workers (Marx's and Lenin's "proletariat") were in no way unanimous in wanting collectivism. The more advanced the capitalist economy, the less was the enthusiasm among industrial workers and their intellectual spokesmen, for the dictatorship of the proletariat (Marxism) or of the party leading the proletariat (Leninism), and everything it entailed. In the Soviet Union the suppression of private ownership of property had not led to the spontaneous reorganization of the economy along collectivist lines, and the elimination of material incentives had simply led to a decline of economic activities. Instead of collapsing under the impact of the political and economic postwar crises, democracy (except in Italy and Hungary) had recovered, and it seemed to be gaining ground in non-Western nations.

Leninists maintained that there was nothing wrong with their theory, that at most there had been a misinterpretation of the conditions in "capitalist" (democratic) countries. Still, action had to be adjusted to the reality if the movement was to survive. The political adjustment was simple: within the context of the dictatorship advocated by Marx, and, more clearly, by Lenin, there was a strengthening of despotism in the Soviet Union, and of discipline in the communist movement. The economic adjustment in the country the communists controlled was considerably more difficult: with few exceptions (the most important being the British Fabians) socialists had never been willing to face the concrete problem of the institutional organization of collectivism. Lenin had, in a fumbling way, tried two different approaches (the mixed economy of 1917–1918 and of the NEP, and the so-called war communism) and had failed.

Overworked and exhausted, Lenin had suffered strokes, which by 1923 made it impossible for him to exercise effective leadership; but as long as he was alive no one could replace him. A new situation arose with his death on January 21, 1924. Because of the rigid, disciplined, hierarchical structure of the communist movement, the only people who counted were a few men at the top level of the Soviet Communist party. Among them the most influential were Trotsky, Zinoviev, Kamenev, Bukharin, Rykov, Stalin, and Tomsky. Until Lenin's death, Stalin had been little known, but his position as head of the party organization had already given him greater real power than any of the others enjoyed. With the advantage of hindsight one can say that of the seven men the one who best interpreted Lenin's position was Stalin. Besides the ideology—on which, with some variations (especially on the part of Trotsky), they agreed—what made for Leninism was totalitarianism: total intolerance and total intransigence. Lenin's efforts had been aimed at creating a communist movement that would mirror his own ideological totalitarianism, at making the communist Soviet state a totalitarian state. Through his strong personality Lenin had dominated his collaborators, but not all had shared his totalitarianism. Trotsky had been a good Leninist only temporarily, during the revolution and the civil war; Bukharin, the author of sophomoric writings that had given him the reputation of being "the party's leading theorist," [4] had objected to the suppression of freedom of the press; Zinoviev had gone so far as to express horror for the massacres carried out during the communist Terror; all, at one time or another, had favored alliances, agreements, and coalitions that would have made the realization of the Leninist brand of socialism impossible. Stalin, whatever his own vacillations may have been before April 1917, became the embodiment of totalitarianism, and communism today owes as much to him as to Lenin.

During Lenin's illness, factions had been forming around Trotsky, Zinoviev, Kamenev, Bukharin, and Stalin. Lenin seemed to be aware of what was going on but lacked the strength to intervene. He had become particularly suspicious of Stalin, who had in-

[4] I. Deutscher, *The Prophet Unarmed* (London: Oxford University Press, 1959), p. 82.

sulted his wife. In his so-called testament, a letter addressed in December 1922 to the party congress, he vaguely advocated "collective leadership," which was tried, but did not function successfully either then or in 1953–1957. After Lenin's death factionalism erupted, although at the time little was publicly known about what was actually going on. For some, the conflict—which affected the communist movement everywhere—was an ideological one; for others it was a sordid competition for power. Both elements existed and it is difficult to separate them. There were dissensions on internal and external questions: on the NEP, policies towards the peasantry, the attitude to be adopted toward other socialist movements and toward nonsocialist movements, the timing of revolutionary activities, the choice between all-out revolutionary efforts or a cautious, long-range policy, the technique of industrialization.

In a series of lectures delivered in 1924, Stalin described his position clearly. "Objective: to consolidate the dictatorship of the proletariat in one country, using it as a base for the overthrow of imperialism in all countries. . . . Main forces . . .: the dictatorship of the proletariat in one country, the revolutionary movement of the proletariat in all countries. Main reserves: the semiproletarian and small-peasant masses in the developed countries, the liberation movement in the colonies and dependent countries. . . . Direction of the main blow: isolation of the democrats." The most difficult of the problems was industrialization.

Many communists and most noncommunists had taken for granted that Trotsky would be Lenin's successor. Trotsky himself confidently expected this to be the case. His main opponent was Zinoviev, the head of the Comintern. In the Political Bureau of the Communist party of the Soviet Union (CPSU), the supreme organ after Lenin's death, Zinoviev, supported by Kamenev, sided with Stalin and Rykov against Trotsky. The main point of dissension was the issue, debated since 1921, of world revolution versus socialism in one country. Trotsky became the embodiment of the principle of world revolution. Of course there was more: Trotsky's ideological position was not identical with that of his opponents in the CPSU. He became increasingly isolated. The man who, according to many admirers, had "laid the foundation of what had arisen in Russia" and who had declared "we will deal with the enemies with an iron hand," saw the iron hand being applied to himself.

Having isolated Trotsky, Stalin dropped the alliance with Zinoviev, Kamenev, and Radek, supposedly on the issue of industrialization, and made an agreement with Bukharin, which had the support also of Rykov, the prime minister of the Soviet Union, and Tomsky, the able organizer of the Soviet labor unions. Fearful of losing all influence, Zinoviev and Kamenev allied themselves with Trotsky and tried to organize their own faction within the party. In 1927, when party officials who owed their jobs to Stalin had chosen all the delegates to the 15th party congress, Trotsky, Zinoviev, and Kamenev decided to appeal to the rank and file of the party. The demonstration was met with indifference by the Moscow workers, and Trotsky, the man to whom, next to Lenin, the revolution owed the most, was sent into exile in Soviet central Asia. Around the internal issue of the collectivization of agriculture—actually the exploitation of the peasantry for the purpose of building up an industrial system rapidly—dissension arose between Stalin, advocate of total and swift collectivization, and Bukharin, supported by Rykov and Tomsky. When the 6th world congress of the Communist International opened in 1928, Bukharin "remorseful for what he had done to Trotsky and even more dreading the new Genghiz Khan" [5] unavailingly quoted a letter sent him by Lenin: "If you chase all intelligent people who are not very pliable, and only keep obedient idiots, then you will certainly ruin the party." [6] Bukharin and his friends ceased to count in the party, and he lingered for a few more years until finally arrested and executed during the great purges.

The bitter factionalism within the communist leadership during the middle twenties was the outcome of dogmatism—as the conflict between Stalinists and Titoists in 1948, and between Khrushchevites and Maoists in the sixties were to be. There were differences, of course, but they were magnified by the rigidity of ideological positions. With the help of hindsight again one can say that, from a communist point of view, Stalin was generally right. For a long time Stalinists and Trotskyites, the two main opposing factions, hated each other more than they hated capitalism or democratic socialism. But the factionalism influenced the movement profoundly, and the triumph of the Stalinists helped to give it the characteristics by which we know it today.

The same process, aiming at the elimination of all opposition, nonconformity, or deviation from the party line, went on during that period in the communist movement in the rest of Europe and outside Europe. The twenty-one points approved by the 2d world congress of the Communist International had been clear enough. Had there been less intransigence, it is likely that a larger number of people would have joined the communist parties of the various countries at that time. This would have led to a dilution of basic communist characteristics. In Germany, for instance,

[5] I. Deutscher, *op. cit.*, p. 469.
[6] F. Borkenau, *op. cit.*, p. 337.

out of 800,000 Independent Socialists, only 300,000
decided to join the Communist party, originally organized around the 50,000 Spartacists. But the smaller
numbers were more than offset by greater cohesion.
The struggle for leadership in the party between
Brandler, Maslow, Fischer, Thaelmann ended with the
victory of the latter, who had followed the Stalinist
line closely from the beginning and had unconditionally accepted the open letter from the Comintern to
the German Communist party on the need for absolute
allegiance to the Soviet Union.

In France many socialists (Froissard, Souvarine, and
others) who had enthusiastically embraced the communist cause and had been responsible for the split
in the French Socialist party in 1920, abandoned
communism. In Italy, the group led by Bordiga was
expelled from the party, which was dominated by the
Stalinist Togliatti (1893–   ). The Norwegian group
under Traenmel left the Comintern as early as 1923.
In Poland the majority of the not numerous communists had taken their inspiration from Rosa Luxemburg and from Radek: they were expelled from the
party, and those who were in the Soviet Union perished
in the later purges.

As far as the movement was concerned, Stalinism
meant the strengthening of its monolithic character,
which had been one of Lenin's main goals. This was
one of Stalin's major contributions to the development
of communism. Factional strife, ending in the expulsion of non-Stalinists, occurred in all non-European
communist parties. In the areas controlled by Chinese
communists expulsion often meant execution.

Monolithic Organization

The communist movement as it exists today was
molded during that troubled period beginning with

the year of revolution and ending with the consolidation of Stalin's control in 1927. Since 1956–1957 it has become polycentric. But each of the autonomous sections into which communism is divided is what Lenin wanted the Russian Bolsheviki to be: a highly disciplined movement with a maximum of cohesion achieved through rigid centralization of authority and the elimination of all internal differences and conflicts.

The system of organization was described in party circles as "democratic centralism." This term meant that discipline flowed downwards, every party organ being subordinated to the organ above it and ultimately to the central committee. What happened between 1917 and 1927 was simply the logical development of so-called democratic centralism. The leaders used their authority to eliminate from the communist parties all who did not agree with their policies, and the parties were reduced to mirrors that reflected the leaders' will, aspirations, and policies. The process by which discipline flows downwards guarantees a maximum of cohesion. A communist party can be joined only by those who are willing to submerge their personalities completely in the anonymous mass of loyal and faithful followers, and who accept totally the "line" determined by the leaders. The efficiency of the communist parties derives to a large extent from the fact that they are not political parties in the usual meaning of the term. They represent an all-embracing way of life: joining the party is an experience equivalent to joining a church in times of great religious fervor.

The organization of a communist party is relatively simple. Anyone who unconditionally accepts the principles of Marxism-Leninism in the interpretation given by the leaders may join. However, to make sure that applicants are genuinely convinced and that they possess the animus required of party members, acceptance in the party is preceded everywhere by a probationary period, usually lasting several years. The basic elements are the cells, consisting of communists who work in the same place (factory, mine, office, farm, and so forth) or who live in the same neighborhood. Party members meet and discuss problems at the level of cells. There are several hundred thousands of these primary or local groups in the Soviet Union; no figures are available on the number of cells outside the Soviet Union. Contacts between cells are few; those that do exist are rigidly controlled by the cell leader; hence it is extremely difficult, nay impossible, for any party member to look for other fellow-members whose cooperation would be required to start a movement within the party. Through their leaders cells are grouped into district, provincial, or regional units, and these in turn into national parties. On the national level, authority is exercised nominally by central executive committees, but in reality—at least since 1926—by presidiums or politburos. These were patterned on the Political Bureau of the Russian Communist party, established in 1917, to become, in 1919, the supreme political organ.

As long as the Communist International existed, all national parties were subject to it. The Comintern was an emanation of the Politburo of the CPSU and exercised its authority through an executive committee that functioned permanently. After the dissolution of the Comintern (1943) and until 1956, the functions of the committee were exercised by the Politburo (later Presidium) of the CPSU in collaboration with a few outstanding communist leaders outside the Soviet Union. Since 1956–1957 meetings of representatives of communist parties have been used to maintain the cohesion of the communist movement. Because cohesion was weakening in the early 1960s, meetings of representatives of communist parties have ensured unity of directives and policies for the major divisions within communism.

Democratic centralism has taken the form of hierarchical authoritarianism, through the application of a simple formula: leaders originally self-appointed and, as time goes on and vacancies occur, co-opted by those already in the leadership, determine who is to be in the rank and file; then the rank and file goes through the motion of electing the leaders who are already there or have been co-opted. The will of the leadership is the same as the will of the rank and file. In democratic procedure, the membership chooses the leadership; in communist procedure, the leadership chooses the membership. There may be dissident communists outside the party, but there is no room for a dissident communist within it. Once the dissident has been expelled from the party he can exert no influence. Only at the top level of leadership (the Politburo or Presidium) is there at any time a possibility for individual expression of opinion or for independence. Divisions within communism come from above, never —so far—from the rank and file.

The main function of the communist parties is to exercise dictatorial powers. Sympathizers and critics have recognized that this is the main feature of the political structure of the Soviet Union. The Webbs wrote, for instance: "The administration of the U.S.S.R. is controlled to an extent which . . . it would be hard to exaggerate by the Communist Party." What, since the end of 1917, had been the position of the Communist party in Russia has become the position of the communist parties in all the countries in which they have been able to seize political power.

There is considerable difference of opinion on the

internal freedom within a communist party. For some "there is . . . opportunity for critical discussion regarding the effectiveness of shortcomings of the administration. . . . Major decisions of social policy are frequently preceded by widespread public discussions. . . . When the decision has been made . . . freedom of discussion in regard to the decision itself is considered at an end." But Borkenau, who has been intimately connected with the communist organization, wrote: "Since 1925 policy and administration became centralized in a few hands . . . since 1925 the central committees of the communist parties had been replaced by political bureaus in which the critical tendencies within the parties had no longer a voice . . . the autonomy of regions and districts was curtailed to the point of annihilation . . . the active membership was deprived, as early as 1926, of any possibility of exerting in practice its right to participate in the laying down of party policy."

Whatever the opinion of communist sympathizers, it can be said that, as the result of expelling (or liquidating) those who disagree with the decisions of the party leadership, there is no internal freedom within communist parties. In those countries where a communist party can make use of the state authority for its own aims, the freedom of the communists within a communist organization is as limited as the freedom of the noncommunists outside. The intransigence, which, in the early phase of the movement, communists displayed towards noncommunists, has been transferred to the communists themselves. Concerning the internal organization, it is necessary to recognize that the concentration of power in the hands of a few individuals with full authority over their followers helped the movement to achieve considerable flexibility of action. This flexibility is particularly useful when accompanied by a correct evaluation of the situation at any given moment.

Marxism-Leninism supplies the intelligentsia—since the beginning in 1903 the dynamic element in the communist movement—with an easy explanation for all phenomena, human and nonhuman, past, present, and future. The principles mentioned in previous sections of this chapter are reinterpreted with slight variations, additions, and corrections by those who happen to be, at one time or another, in one country or another, omnipotent leaders. But the principles form an unchanging core. They furnish a justification for whatever line of conduct has been adopted, and provide each individual communist with an intellectual armor solid enough to make him impervious to criticism. The importance of this armor in the overall picture of communist strength should not be underestimated. The evidence gathered by the communist intellectuals to support their arguments, which is accepted uncritically by the rank and file, and the logic of their reasoning exert a considerable influence in providing the communist movement with a uniformity little affected by factional divisions.

Communists pride themselves on their rationality. Actually, as with all fanatics, there is a good deal of irrationality in communist thinking. Faith, more than reason, provides communists with the coherent thought that most men need in order to face life and its problems. A fallacy in Marxist-Leninist reasoning is to assume in the definition what is to be proved—an ordinary, old-fashioned way of proving that one is always right. A few examples will suffice:

1. "The administrative apparatus of a socialist economy can never become a new ruling class, because it lacks private ownership," wrote E. Browder, a former leader of the

American Communist party, who probably never heard of Praetorians or Mamelukes, among others, all of them propertyless rulers exploiting property-owning classes.

2. Socialism frees man from the bonds originating from economic shortages and economic restrictions; communists compel people to become socialists; *ergo,* communists make people free.

3. Imperialism is a phase of capitalism; communism is the negation of capitalism; therefore a communist state cannot be imperialistic. (Corollary: annexation by a communist state is an act of emancipation).

4. Aggressive war is the outcome of internal conflicts (in capitalistic societies, the variety of interests); there are no internal conflicts in a socialist state; *ergo,* no socialist state can be the aggressor in war. (This argument has been used widely to prove that there was no communist aggression in the cases of Poland and Finland in 1939, of Korea in 1950, of India in 1962.)

This is the kind of reasoning that appeals not only to uneducated communists but also to legions of intellectuals. In analyzing the working of the communist mind, one should not forget that the communists are far from having a monopoly in the use of fallacies: they just do it better. Their exercises in semantics, reminiscent of scholastic practices in the Middle Ages, have helped to break down the barriers that critical faculties may oppose to communist ideology. As happened in the fascist ideology, there is a seemingly strict logical process within the framework of what is basically an irrational system. The irrationality is covered up by faith; the logic satisfies the rational element in the intellectuals, who have played a greater role than the "toiling masses" in the development of the communist movement.

The concept of liberty as the intellectual and political expression of free will is unknown to communists, for whom "individual freedom . . . is conceived in terms of economic security. . . . Equal rights [mean that] . . . Soviet policy does not tolerate dissent in matters of substance. . . . Freedom of the Press means that political powers take over all means of communication and proceed to control them." [7] Communists have a simple and uncritical faith in their system as the gate to the millennium. Their materialism has helped them dispense with ethical principles and freed them from the inhibitions that restrain the actions of most people. But materialism among communists has not led to cynicism; it has strengthened them as only a religious faith could have done.

Communists are fond of stressing that theirs is a new morality. Actually it is a very old one. The main feature of communist morality is the double standard, its main principle the traditional one that the end justifies the means. Under both aspects communism is the negation of the efforts to formulate a higher type of morality made by most religions and by ancient and modern philosophical thought. Because of their concept of what is right and what is wrong, agreements or contracts made with communists have little or no value.

An analysis of the structure of the communist organization explains the institutions introduced by communist parties in the countries where they have seized political power. It would indeed have been strange if the communists had dealt with others more leniently than with themselves! To the hierarchical party corresponds a hierarchical state, all the way from the citizens who are beyond salvation (members

---

[7] *Communism in Action*, Washington, D.C.: U.S. Government Printing Office, 1946, pp. 133ff.

of the *bourgeoisie,* the clergy, the landowning classes, and so forth) and are helped to disappear as quickly as possible, to the citizens who are slow to understand the meaning of salvation (the farmers), those who are saved because of their economic function (industrial workers), and the party members (reliable people whose duty it is to show others the way to salvation and who must report all sinful acts and thoughts). Real democracy means the total transfer of power from the citizens to the rulers. Democratic centralism means the concentration of total power in the hands of rulers, on the assumption that they express the revolutionary will of the triumphant proletariat. Authority from above is identified with authority from below through a combination of fear and bribes, which induce those "below" to agree with those "above." As a communist party eliminates—and liquidates whenever possible—all "deviationists" (only the politburos have, collectively, the right to deviate), so an effort is made through the tools of the police state (arbitrary arrests and trials, firing squads, concentration camps, among other means) to eliminate all expression of dissent. The party functions 100 percent as a single unit; the citizens are regimented through state-controlled organizations in such a way as to function as a single unit. In the communist state all responsibility, all thinking, all decision making is the monopoly of the Politburo. Whatever autonomy individuals may enjoy is a concession made by the leaders, not a right.

C H A P T E R . . . 2

The Middle Period: Stalinism

Collectivism, Consolidation, and Aloofness (1927-1933)

Stalin was the absolute ruler of the Soviet Union and supreme leader of the communist movement from the end of 1927 until his death early in 1953. His image is that of a ruthless dictator, inexorable liquidator of factions, classes and nations, creator of the Soviet empire. During the years of his triumphant successes, communists seized power in fourteen countries and came close to doing so in several others. However, Stalin's greatest and most lasting contribution to communism was the organization of the collectivist economy: what had been an idea that for generations most people thought impractical became a blueprint and then a reality. Lenin had had no clear ideas on the subject of organizing collectivism. Stalin's opponents, brilliant though some of them were, had failed to formulate practical proposals concerning collectivist institutions. Democratic socialists everywhere were uncertain when it came to economic changes, and in most cases restricted themselves to a reform of capitalistic structures.

Stalin was no economist. All he did was to apply Lenin's basic political formulas to the economy. The outcome was the creation *ex novo* of a rigidly hierarchical bureaucratic structure responsible for the total regimentation of labor and of capital, both natural and artificial, and for the management of all economic enterprises; a bureaucratic structure competent to carry out detailed decisions of a supreme economic council receiving orders from and acting under the supervision of the political rulers. It was enough to have bureaucratic regimentation for collectivism to operate. Capital was needed for the expansion of the collectivist economy just as it is needed for the expansion of any economy: by depressing the standards of living of the population, Stalin was able to transform into capital an exceptionally high proportion of labor.[1] It worked, but over ten years had passed since the revolution before Stalin's collectivism got under way early in 1928. Communists who were to seize power in other countries could begin immediately where Stalin had started and, with the benefit of Soviet experience, could accomplish in a shorter period what had been achieved in the Soviet Union.

Lenin had seen in the development of electricity a main factor of industrialization, and in 1921 a committee was set up to control power plants and the distribution of electricity. That committee had grown

[1] "The source of capital for the rapid development of industry was the labor of the peasant and the worker." L. Shapiro, *The Communist Party of the Soviet Union,* New York: Random House, Inc., 1960, p. 420.

into a central economic commission by 1925 when the 14th congress of the CPSU approved a plan for the industrialization of the country. Under orders from Stalin, the commission, later known as the Gosplan, drafted a blueprint for the whole of the Soviet economy. After the 15th party congress had expelled the Trotsky-Zinoviev group, the first five-year plan was introduced (1928-1932). Stalin was in a hurry. For practical as well as ideological reasons, communism and the Soviet Union needed an expanding collectivist economy.

There was at the time a war scare among the Soviet leaders, probably the result of a number of factors: the anticommunist policy adopted by the British government following the failure of the general strike in 1926; the break between nationalists and communists in China; several minor episodes such as raids against communist headquarters in Germany and the murder of Soviet representatives abroad; the growing strength of anticommunist totalitarian movements (the number of admirers of Italian fascism was growing rapidly). What appeared to be, until 1929, the strengthening of democratic capitalism in North America caused preoccupation for Stalin and his collaborators. Moreover, totalitarianism was the goal to be achieved in what the faithful everywhere called the socialist fatherland, and political despotism cannot become totalitarian unless all economic forces are brought under state control.

A remarkable economic recovery took place in the Soviet Union during the seven years of the NEP (1921–1927). By the end of 1927 the economic wounds caused by the war, the revolution, and the civil war had been healed, and production restored to the level of 1913 when Russia was fifth in importance among the industrial countries of the world. But the recovery strengthened the economic position of groups of the population that were not in sympathy with communist ideals and practices. From the standpoint of Marxism-Leninism a threat to the solidity of the regime was implicit in the recovery. Furthermore, Stalin and his supporters were convinced that the successful collectivization of the Soviet Union would increase the appeal of communism everywhere, to the detriment not only of Western liberal democracy, which stood for free enterprise, but also of democratic socialism, which was gaining ground in Great Britain, Scandinavia, Australia, India, and other countries, and which then stood for a mixed economy based on planning and limited nationalization.

Stalin had stated that the USSR was fifty to one hundred years behind the advanced countries, that an effort had to be made to close the gap in just ten years. The organs entrusted with economic planning became, next to the secret police, the most important element in the administration of the country. Little opposition could be expected in the industrial and commercial fields, where all large concerns had been nationalized before 1921 and where the remaining small independent industrialists, craftsmen, and shopkeepers were easily absorbed into state-controlled organizations. More opposition was anticipated from the peasants, who, from the beginning, had shown greater sympathy for the Socialist Revolutionaries than for the communists. They considered themselves owners of the soil and still formed by far the largest section of the population of the Soviet Union. Among them, the prosperous farmers (Kulaks) represented about 1 million households, or a little over 5 million persons. They were not landlords, or landowners, but peasants who sometimes (not always) received the additional help of hired labor. Their wealth (a better house, a few more acres of land, some livestock) was little according to Western standards, but considerable according to those of the other peasants.

On January 5, 1930, the party leaders decided to eliminate the Kulaks. In what was a mass persecution, millions of people were uprooted. Most ended in the forced labor camps of northern Russia and eastern Siberia. Those who protested were jailed; many were shot. The party acted so efficiently and ruthlessly that two months later Stalin was able to call a halt to the process of elimination. But the result was felt in the diminishing agricultural returns that year and in the years following, and in the famine that caused a decline in the population of several areas of the Soviet Union. Two important goals had been achieved, however. Young peasants began to move in increasing numbers to the mining areas and the cities, providing badly needed, even if unskilled, industrial labor. More important, a large proletariat that provided cheap labor for basic but often unprofitable industries was collected in convict labor camps.

The first five-year plan was followed by the second. The physical aspect of the Soviet Union began to change. With the technical help of several thousand foreign engineers (mostly Germans and Americans) and foreign machinery paid for with the commodities the peasants had been deprived of, coal, iron, and oil fields were better exploited. The output of electricity increased. New factories were set up, and to the prerevolution industrial areas of Leningrad, Moscow, and southern European Russia, others were added on the Volga east of Moscow, in the Urals, in Transcaucasia, and in western and central Siberia (later also in central Asia and the Siberian Far East). The population of Moscow, Leningrad, and many other cities increased considerably. Rail and water transportation were improved. Special attention was paid to the development of scientific and technological research centers. The results of Soviet collectivism from the inception of the first five-year plan to the German invasion of June 1941 have inspired differing appraisals. Typical of the enthusiasm for Soviet achievements was the statement of an American communist (who later recanted) Earl Browder (1891–   ). He wrote that "during the First Five-Year Plan, the rate of increase in industrial production averaged 22 percent annually." A contrary view was, for instance, that of an expert in Russian affairs, L. Schwarzschild, who stated that "the ratio between Soviet and American rates of growth in equivalent decades is 70 to 96 in iron, 588 to 1,389 in coal, 410 to 1,598 in copper, 38 to 1,320 in railroad construction, and so on."

The first Soviet economic achievements came at a time when the American and western European economies had been severely hit by the great depression of 1929–1933. They were highly publicized and struck the imagination of people who lacked the necessary information to make a comparison between Soviet and other economies. Figures about unemployment in the United States and Europe were available, but figures about the millions in forced labor camps in the Soviet Union were either unavailable or could not be proved officially. Soviet figures concerning production were vague and often contradictory. It took a long time to get a clear, accurate picture of the Soviet economy. It can be said now that Soviet achievements in 1928–1941 were remarkable, but in no way superior to those obtained in several free enterprise North American and European countries during the corresponding phase of industrial development. During that phase the Soviet over-all rate of economic growth was no greater than what it had been during the last few years in pre-1914 Russia. Moreover, growth was

Joseph Stalin. *(U.S. Army Photo)*

very uneven, with mining and heavy industry in the
lead and agriculture lagging; light industries, construction, and transportation occupied a middle position.
But the results were sufficient to justify the satisfaction
felt by Stalin and his close economic collaborators,
Kuibyshev (1888–1935), Voznesensky (1903–1950),
Kaganovich (1893–   ), Mikoyan (1895–   ). Through
able propaganda that intelligently exploited a number
of motives—from love of fatherland to fear, from devotion to an ideal to greed—a state of psychosis was
maintained that induced large sections of the population to accept willingly the harsh tyranny and the
privations required for the execution of the five-year
plans.

The consolidation of Stalin's despotic power, the
establishment of economic collectivism, and the fast-
growing tension in international affairs in the thirties
were all factors in the final liquidation of internal
opposition in the Soviet Union. The assassination of
Kirov (1886–1934), the party leader in the Leningrad
area, supposedly a trusted collaborator of Stalin and,
from a communist point of view, something of a
moderate, served as pretext for launching a campaign
to destroy opponents and would-be opponents. Secret
police and public prosecutors had a free hand. Those
who had been Lenin's closest collaborators during the
first six years of the communist dictatorship were tried
and condemned to death. Thousands of their followers
(for instance, those who had been oppositionists with
Trotsky and Zinoviev in 1927) were shot. Forced labor
camps, emptied of the peasants who had filled them
in 1930, were filled again—to the advantage of the
economy. The famous secret report of 1956 on the
crimes of the Stalin era mentions only a fraction of
the atrocities that it is now known were carried out
at the time. Besides the execution of the Old Bolshe-

viki, what impressed most foreigners was the purge
in the armed forces, where "the total number of
victims, according to a Japanese intelligence estimate,
was 35,000 in all, or about half of the officer corps." [2]
Estimates of the victims of the purges made at the
time proved to be well below the actual numbers.
These may have been as high as about 300,000 executed and 7 million arrested.[3]

The official communist view was that "the trials
showed that these dregs of humanity . . . had been in
conspiracy against Lenin, the Party, and the Soviet
state ever since the early days of the October Socialist
Revolution." [4] Party members and fellow-travelers
justified this spectacular series of treason trials on the
grounds that elimination of opposition was required
in order to strengthen the Soviet Union militarily, in
view of the growing tension caused by the rise of
fascism. A simpler explanation is that it is in the
nature of totalitarianism to destroy what cannot be
assimilated as soon as it is strong enough to do so.
By the middle 1930s communism and Stalinism were
one: anti-Stalinist communists, real or imaginary, were
crushed as forcibly as anticommunists had been during
Dzierzynski's terror; loyal Stalinists were executed because Stalin had become suspicious of them. Whatever
the explanation, there is no doubt that by 1938 all
organized opposition within the CPSU and all potential opposition outside it in the Soviet Union had
been efficiently destroyed. Soviet communism had
finally achieved the monolithic strength that is the
concomitant of the exercise of absolute power con-

[2] *Ibid.*, p. 420.

[3] This is the estimate made by G. Dickler, *Man on Trial,* New
York: Doubleday & Company, Inc., 1962, p. 262.

[4] Official *History of the Communist Party of the Soviet Union,*
New York: International Publishers Co., Inc., 1939, p. 347.

centrated in the hands of a few leaders. Politically as well as economically Stalin had completed Lenin's work.

There was one point on which Stalin may be said to have differed, practically if not ideologically, from Lenin's position. He was less of a genuine internationalist than either Lenin or any other communist leader prominent in the 1917–1927 period. The essay on *The Problems of Nationalities and Social Democracy,* written in 1912, had given him a reputation as an expert on national questions. Partly because of this and partly because of his Georgian origins, he had been appointed commissar for the nationalities in 1917. He had been instrumental in establishing the Soviet system among the ethnic minorities in the Russian territories reoccupied by the communists in 1918–1922. However, through conviction or opportunism, he soon identified himself with Great Russian nationalism.[5] This identification probably facilitated the formulation of the Stalinist slogan "socialism in one country," just as Trotsky's internationalism was a natural foundation for the policy of world revolution. The triumph of the faction led by Stalin was at least partly responsible for the contradiction, in Marxist-Leninist terminology, between nationalism and internationalism, which a few decades later led to the development of national-communism and polycentrism.

Stalin's victory in the CPSU had had repercussions in all communist parties and had been accompanied by the expulsion of rightist and leftist deviationists, as they were called, who had not recanted in time. This, together with the application of the twenty-one points of 1920, had limited the number of card-bearing

[5] I. Deutscher, *Stalin, A Political Biography,* New York: Oxford University Press, 1949, pp. 240-244.

members of the communist parties. Still, the secretary-general of the Comintern was able to state at the 6th world congress of the organization (July-September 1928), that the total membership of the sixty-six parties represented was about 4 million. Deducting the 700,000 of the CPSU, there remained over 3 million for the rest of the world. Of them, the largest group, approximately one tenth of the total, was in Germany. In relation to the world population 3 million might seem an insignificant minority, but they formed a highly cohesive group which an able and aggressive leadership could maneuver at will. No other organization at that time had so many disciplined and dedicated members. Lenin's policy of intransigence was to pay good dividends, and it saved the communist movement from the weakness that internal divisions caused among the other branches of the socialist movement.

The tactical retreat initiated at the end of 1923 continued in Europe from 1927–1934. There was a lessening of overt revolutionary activity. Each party's preoccupation was to strengthen its own organization by the purging of all dissident, dubious, or weak elements, and by an intensive effort toward ideological clarification. Each member had to know exactly what communism was and what his obligations were. At the same time, communists everywhere kept aloof from contacts with members of other movements. It was their duty to detach themselves entirely from everyone else, but now the main object of their hatred was the democratic socialists. Long since, Engels had maintained that "from the first moment of victory . . . the distrust of the workers must not be directed against the conquered reactionary party but against the . . . *bourgeois* democrats." After the profound transformation brought about in the socialist movement by the crises of World War I and the Soviet revolution, everywhere in Europe socialists, that is, members of parties affiliated to the Second International, had become the strongest supporters of democratic institutions. In his lectures in 1924 Stalin had stated that the communists' main enemy was now "the parties of the Second International. . . . The mortal sin of the Second International was . . . that it overestimated the importance of the parliamentary forms of struggle, that it considered them virtually the only form." [6] Communists everywhere decided to do, before the ultimate victory, what Engels had advised to do only afterwards, thus confirming what the German socialdemocratic leader Kautsky said of them: "the fundamental aim of the communists is . . . the destruction of democracy." Communists attached particular importance to their future success in Germany and France: they hated the German Weimar Republic and the French Third Republic more than any other political entity. (Heirs to that hatred were first Great Britain and then, from the beginning of 1945, the United Sates.)

Engels' "reactionary party" was represented in Europe, in the years when Stalin was achieving power, by rightist antidemocratic regimes. The communists' opposition to democracy led them to work on lines parallel to those of the rightist enemies of democracy. This happened in 1920 in Germany when Kapp revolted against the Weimar Republic. It happened in Italy when fascists seized power (October 1922), and later in 1924 when the communists refused to make common cause with the socialists, liberals, and democratic Catholics who were trying to stem the tide of the fascist movement. It happened again when Zankoff and his Macedonian followers rose in Bulgaria against

[6] J. Stalin, *Foundations of Leninism,* New York: International Publishers Co., Inc., 1939, p. 89.

the agrarian leader Stamboliiski (1923), and in Poland when Pilsudski overthrew the democratic regime (1926). In France, in 1927–1928, the communists (from whose ranks all non-Stalinists had been eliminated) decided to drop the electoral collaboration that had existed previously with the socialists and liberals (Radical Socialists), and helped the right to gain greater electoral successes. Under the leadership of Thaelmann and Neumann, the German communists worked after 1928 along lines parallel to the fascists of the National Socialist party. They hailed as their own victory the elimination of the socialdemocrats from the government of Prussia in 1932, a prelude to the fascist seizure of power in Germany a few months later.

In the two non-European countries (the United States and China) where communism had achieved a modest intellectual and political significance before the Comintern adopted its policy of aloofness, the opening years of the Stalinist era coincided in both cases with a strengthening of the movement. This was the result of its appeal among fringe intellectuals and pseudointellectuals in the United States, and of a tactical retreat in China. The importance of the communist infatuation of sectors of the American intelligentsia in the thirties (and in the forties: it lasted until approximately 1948) should not be exaggerated, nor should the number of people involved. But infatuation there was, linked on one hand to the economic and social crisis that accompanied the depression of 1929–1933, and on the other to a near-total ignorance of what was happening in the Soviet Union. Most of the American so-called communists in the thirties were rather naive people of goodwill who did not understand that totalitarianism (which they hated) was implicit in Leninist ideology and inherent in Soviet institutions.

In China, after the triumph of the nationalist faction in the Kuomintang in 1927 and the expulsion of Soviet agents, a few centers of communist resistance were set up in various parts of the country (in the counties on the border between Hunan and Kiangsi, in the hilly areas where the provinces of Anwei, Honan, and Hupeh meet, in the northwestern provinces). The Kuomintang armies tried to occupy the communist-controlled areas. Under the leadership of Mao Tse-tung and Chu-Teh, in October 1934 the communists south of the Yangtze Kiang began the "long march," which ended a year later in the northern province of Shensi. There, at Yenan, they established headquarters, reorganized the party, formed their own administration, and carried out intermittent warfare against the nationalists, who had been pressed by Japanese attacks since 1931. After a severe factional squabble during which emerged for brief periods first Ch'u Ch'iu-pai (1899–1935) and then Li Li-san (1886–   ), complete control over the party was achieved by Mao in 1932. His victory over the opposition was the equivalent of Stalin's victory in the Soviet Union five years before. Mao's party was not controlled by Soviet agents as most other communist parties were. All the same, it was considered to be a loyal Stalinist party.

It was during the opening years of the Stalinist era that communism expanded enough to be able to shed its European character. Until then communism had been a movement that had happened to triumph in the eastern section of the Continent, spreading to some extent to North America and China, but aiming basically at the collectivization, according to Marxist-Leninist principles, of the advanced industrial economies of western and central Europe. By the late twenties and early thirties communist groups began to count politically in Latin America and Asia (out-

side China). Everywhere they lacked a mass base. Those
who embraced communism were intellectuals and
semi-intellectuals, but they were numerous enough
and active enough to form politically influential
groups; they were no longer just a few isolated individuals.

In Latin America, considerable influence was exercised by the communists in Mexico, where they merged
in the triumphant agrarianism and anticlericalism of
the 1928–1940 period. In Cuba, the communists' action
against Grau San Martin in 1933 was parallel to that
of the Americans and of Batista. In Chile, communists,
including distinguished intellectuals, vigorously opposed the democratic socialists. In Venezuela and in
Peru communists were the main opponents of, respectively, the Democratic Alliance and the APRA. In
Brazil they were for *Getulismo* and welcomed the
establishment of a near-fascist dictatorship. Bitter
antagonism between Stalinists and Trotskyites weakened the communists in Argentina and Uruguay,
where, as in Chile, they also met with the opposition
of a relatively strong democratic socialist movement.
Trotsky found a number of admirers in Bolivia, where
a Trotskyist party played a political role.

In Asia, communist parties were founded in Annam
(Vietnam) and in the Philippines in 1930, in Ceylon
in 1932. Dutch communists helped to reorganize and
strengthen the Indonesian Communist party in 1935.
A communist party based on the Chinese section of
the population operated in British Malaya. The influence of Gandhi in one case, and of extreme nationalism in another, checked the growth of communism in
India and Japan, although in both countries many
intellectuals looked admiringly at the Soviet Union.
Through the intermediary of the French Communist
party, communism made its appearance in the Arab

countries of the Middle East and North Africa, then controlled by the French. Active communist cells were established in the cities of Syria, Lebanon, Algeria.

The Rise of Fascism and the Phase of Popular Fronts (1934-1939)

Chronologically, the fascist movement in Europe developed after the communist movement. It came into existence largely as an expression of the fear generated in many classes of the population by the triumph of the Bolsheviki in Russia and their reign of terror. Fascists maintained that communism had been bred by liberalism and that parliamentarianism facilitated its spread. Hence they turned even more violently against liberalism and democracy than against communism.

In March 1919 in Milan, Italy's chief industrial city, a small group of people of various political tendencies formed a union, or *fascio*. Insignificant during the first two years, it soon grew so strong that its leader, Benito Mussolini (1883–1945), was able with a show of force to seize the government of Italy (October 1922). After a short experiment in coalition and a violent struggle against their opponents during which several thousand people were killed, the fascists established a totalitarian regime in November 1926. The name *fascism* was given to similar movements that soon developed in various European countries, and later in countries of other continents.

The fascists had a good deal in common with the communists: contempt for parliamentary procedure and for democracy; conviction that their movement was entitled to make use of ruthless violence to achieve its aims; policies leading to the strengthening of the state through the elimination of all dissent and opposi-

tion. They also shared the concept that the group (to
the fascists this meant the nation, not the class) had
complete priority over the individual. They differed
from the communists mainly on economic policies
and, theoretically at least, on the question of nationalism versus internationalism. The fascists were frankly
totalitarian. In Italy as well as in Germany they came
chiefly from the ranks of the lower middle classes
(which in some European countries constitute as much
as one third of the population). These had not participated in the struggle for freedom during the nineteenth century, and newly acquired education had
developed a strong nationalistic feeling among them.
If the lower middle classes provided most of the human
element for the development of fascism, members of
capitalistic groups were generous in providing financial
assistance for a movement that claimed to protect
private ownership of property and stressed order.

The triumph of the fascists in Italy was followed
by the establishment of a military dictatorship in
Spain (1923), by the seizure of power by Pilsudski
(always more of a nationalist that a socialist) in Poland
(1926), by the development of the movement of the
Heimswehr in Austria (1927), and by the establishment of a royal dictatorship in Yugoslavia (1929).
Other fascist or semifascist dictatorships had seized
power in Lithuania (1923) and Portugal (1926). The
Hungarian regime was considered by supporters and
opponents to be close to fascism. In Germany the
first feeble attempts (1923) on the part of the local
fascists (the National Socialists or Nazis) failed misera-
bly, and for several years nazism vegetated obscurely
as one of the many extremist groups in the country;
the economic depression of the early 1930s gave impetus to the movement, and it came into power on
January 30, 1933. The establishment or consolidation

of dictatorships of the right in every country east of Germany and Italy followed, from Estonia to Greece, with the one exception of Czechoslovakia. In the thirties, fascist movements grew rapidly in Far Eastern, Middle Eastern, and Latin American countries. The army and navy officers who ended party government in Japan and finally established a military regime took European fascism as their example. The Brazilian Green Shirts were modeled on European fascist Black and Brown Shirts.

The rise of fascism did not at first unduly worry the communist leaders, who saw in it another enemy of the hated democratic regime. According to the Marxist-Leninist historical scheme, fascism was the last desperate effort of a few capitalists to save their wealth. It should have been a minority movement with no mass appeal. The growth of national socialism in Germany compelled the communists to revise their evaluation of fascism and to recognize the mass appeal of extreme nationalism combined with policies of social reform. In the free elections of the early 1930s, the number of communist voters had increased in Germany from 3 to 6 million. But the number of nazi voters had increased from less than 1 million in 1928 to over 14 million in 1932, and in the presidential elections of that year Adolf Hitler (1889–1945) received 17 million votes. Fascism was no longer the political expression of a frightened minority of property owners. Fascism could be as much of a mass movement as communism, or more.

Stalin and his collaborators realized the danger. The result was a policy change of fundamental importance: "Instead of class struggle, co-operation with the *bourgeoisie*. Instead of the Soviet system, eulogy of democracy. Instead of internationalism, nationalism." To symbolize the change in policy, the leading posi-

tion in the Comintern, occupied since the expulsion
of Bukharin first by Molotov (1890–   ), then by
Manuilsky (1883–1959), was filled by G. Dimitrov
(1882–1949). He was the Bulgarian hero of the *Reich-
stag* fire trial in 1933 (after World War II, dictator of
Bulgaria). During the years 1934–1939, communist
opposition to fascism took precedence over opposition
to democracy.

First came agreements between the Soviet Union
and other countries like France and Czechoslovakia,
and the Soviet Union's application for membership
in the League of Nations (1934). This was followed,
on the national level in various countries, by a reversal of the policy of aloofness and an attempt to
develop "popular fronts" in collaboration with socialist
parties and progressive nonsocialist parties. In France,
communists and socialists had already participated
in joint demonstrations on February 12, 1934—at the
time when the Republic was threatened by rightist
organizations. By 1935 there was collaboration between
socialist and communist youth organizations and trade
unions. When, in 1935, noncommunists launched the
idea of a popular front in France, the Communist
party accepted it enthusiastically, and the result was
the leftist electoral victory of 1936. In Spain, where
the military dictatorship of De Rivera had been replaced by a republican regime, the initial opposition
of the communists to a popular front was quickly
reversed, and there, too, 1936 saw an electoral victory
for the left. The popular-front policy was rejected in
countries where the socialist parties were controlled
by liberal-minded groups (Scandinavia, Great Britain,
Holland), and by the democratic and pacifist socialists
who earlier had formed the Second-and-a-half International. Elsewhere the popular front became a reality.
In dictatorial countries it led to agreements between

communist and socialist undergrounds, or exiles, who were often joined by the radical wing of the middle-class liberal movement.

The Spanish Civil War (July 1936–March 1939) provided a testing ground for the effectiveness of the popular-front policy and for the ability of the communists to take over the leadership of a coalition of which they were part. At the time of the rising in the Asturias (northern Spain) against the Republican government in 1934, communists and some authoritarian socialists collaborated. It was then that Dolores Ibarruri, known as *La Pasionaria,* acquired the reputation that made her one of the leading communists in the world. At the elections of February 1936 the communists had only a few deputies elected in the popular-front list. But after the nationalist rising the Spanish Communist party probably did more, in relation to its small numbers, than any other political group to organize resistance against the military leaders supported by the Catholic hierarchy, the landowners, the majority of the peasantry of western Spain, the Moors from Spanish Morocco, and the German and Italian fascist governments. While fighting against the troops of General F. Franco (1892–   ), the communists tried at the same time to eliminate all opposition to themselves in Republican territory. In clashes that occurred in March 1937 in Barcelona, a number of anarchosyndicalists were killed in addition to many members of the anticommunist socialist group, the Unified Marxist Workers' Party (P.O.U.M.). The Communist party's position in Spain was strengthened by the failure of the French and British governments to help the noncommunist enemies of the nationalists, and by the material help sent by the Soviet Union to the armed forces of the Spanish Republic. The communists organized most of the international brigades that played a prominent part in the defense of the capital and provided valuable fighting experience for communists from all over Europe. The Republic was ultimately defeated, but communist prestige had increased.

The renewal of Japanese attacks against China in 1937 had, for the Chinese communists, an effect similar to that of the triumph of nazism for European communists. They decided to modify their opposition to the nationalists and to build a common front against Japanese militarism, then the Far Eastern equivalent of European fascism. Attempts at cooperation between communists and nationalists increased after the clashes between Japanese and Russian troops along the Manchurian border in 1938. Actively engaged in guerrilla warfare in Japanese-held areas of China, communists strengthened their military organization and won to their side sections of the intelligentsia and the peasantry.

Neutrality (1939-1941)

The popular-front experiment had not been an unqualified success. In Spain it had strengthened the communists for a while, but it had also deepened the cleavage between communists and noncommunist antifascists (democrats, socialdemocrats, syndicalists, anarchosyndicalists, and others). In France it fizzled out after the one-year cabinet (1936–1937) of the socialist Léon Blum. Nowhere in the countries of central and eastern Europe had it shaken the dominant dictatorships of the right.

From a communist viewpoint, there had been several main failures. Popular fronts had not checked the advance of fascism in Europe; at the beginning of 1939, out of twenty-seven European states west of the Soviet

Union, fifteen, with nearly 250 million inhabitants, were under fascist or semifascist dictatorships. Popular fronts had not enabled the various communist parties to dictate their own policy to the parties with which they collaborated; if anything, lack of confidence in the communists had increased. In the international field the policy of collective security through the League of Nations, carried out by the Commissar for Foreign Affairs, M. Litvinov (1876–1951), had not improved relations between the Soviet Union and the two main states of western Europe, the United Kingdom and France. Outside Europe, fascism was expanding rapidly. At the Munich conference (September 1938) the fate of Czechoslovakia, a state considered friendly to the Soviet Union and the only surviving European democracy east of Switzerland, had been settled by the governments of Germany, Italy, France, and Great Britain without so much as an invitation to the Soviet government to be present.

According to Marxist-Leninist theory, "capitalist" countries should have combined in an attack against the socialist state, in this particular case, the Soviet Union. The communist leaders once more proved their flexibility and practicality in action by "freeing" the Germans for a war against Great Britain and France. While a British military mission sent to Moscow in the summer of 1939 was making no headway, conversations were being carried on by Soviet leaders with representatives of the German government. The conversations led to the mutual nonaggression pact of August 23, 1939. As had been the case before 1934, democracy was again the main enemy. On September 1, 1939, the Germans, freed from the fear of major war on two fronts, attacked Poland and World War II started.

The new orientation of the Soviet Union and of

the communist movement had not come unexpectedly. It did, however, cause a certain amount of tension within the communist parties, and still more among fellow-travelers. There were resignations in countries outside the Soviet Union, but not enough to weaken appreciably the communist parties then waging an intensive campaign against the "imperialistic" war in which France and the British Commonwealth had engaged against Germany. What remained of popular front policy was swept away and the communists reverted everywhere to the pre–1934 policy of virulent attacks against liberal democratic states, particularly against Great Britain, the leader in the anti-German coalition, and against democratic socialists as betrayers of the proletariat.

For the first time since 1922 there was an expansion of the territories ruled by communists. The Soviet Union took advantage of the war to occupy states and parts of states on its European borders. This strengthened the communist positions militarily and economically. On September 17, 1939, Soviet troops invaded Poland. As the result of agreements with the nazis, over half the territory of the former Polish republic with more than one third of the population was annexed to Byelorussia and the Ukraine, two republics of the Soviet Union. In the economic field, the process of sovietization in the Polish areas occupied by the Soviet Union was at first carried out more or less along the lines of the NEP: there was confiscation of large estates but no immediate forcible collectivization of agriculture. Wholesale trade was collectivized, but small traders were allowed to continue their businesses. Many factories were dismantled and the machinery taken to the Soviet Union. All in all, the economy took second place. Class and ethnic liquidation was the main concern.

On November 30, 1939, Soviet troops invaded Finland and met with greater resistance than had been expected. But the war ended on March 2, 1940 with a Soviet victory. Finland gave up some territories which, together with former Russian districts, were erected into a new state of the Soviet Union. In the summer of 1940 Soviet troops invaded the three Baltic republics of Estonia, Latvia, and Lithuania. It was reported then that between 200,000 and 300,000 people had been arrested and sent east to end their lives in forced labor camps. There was later evidence of large-scale massacres. Under the threat of war, Rumania was compelled to surrender the province of Bessarabia and the northern part of Bukovina, where a majority of the population was Ukrainian. These actions were justified in communist eyes by the necessity of strengthening the Soviet Union while the "capitalist" nations were fighting it out.

In the British Commonwealth communist parties were relatively unimportant and did not appreciably weaken the British war effort. In France the Communist party, which by then was polling around 1 million votes, sabotaged French military preparations with determination and success. (The desertion from the army of the communist leader Thorez, 1900–   , was a small but significant episode.) When the Germans invaded Yugoslavia and then Greece (April 1941), the communists of the two countries did not move, and resistance against the invaders was at first carried out mainly by nationalistically-minded members of the ruling classes, with the support of sections of the peasant population.

The switch from an antifascist policy to what amounted to a policy of benevolent neutrality towards German fascism could not weaken the position of the communists in the Soviet Union, because all opinion-making media were operated by the government. Official propaganda stressed the anticapitalistic features of fascist regimes. It also emphasized the annexations of 1939–1940, which satisfied the nationalistic aspirations of the Slavic majority of the population of the USSR. Outside the Soviet Union, small numerical losses were more than offset by increased cohesion within the movement. Party members and sympathizers who had stood the shock of the fascist-communist pact of August 1939 were clearly people in whom the leaders could place unlimited confidence.

The Phase of National Fronts (1941-1945)

The German attack on the Soviet Union (June 22, 1941) and the defeats of the Soviet armies on the eastern front during the first few months of war, caused an abrupt and radical reversal of communist tactics everywhere. The communists feared a Japanese attack against the Soviet Far East, but it did not materialize. This time it was no longer a question of popular fronts, of agreements with other progressive movements, both socialist and nonsocialist. The threat was grave, and the very existence of the Soviet Union was in jeopardy. The communists were now willing to collaborate with anyone who was against the Germans and their allies. The "imperialistic" war waged by Great Britain and her allies became a war for freedom and democracy. Even before Pearl Harbor (December 7, 1941), the attitude of American communists towards the foreign policy of the Roosevelt administration changed radically. After June 22, instead of total opposition there was advocacy of intensive aid to Germany's enemies. National fronts became the slogan. In many countries the communists were instrumental in bringing about close integration of antifascist forces.

In the Soviet Union concessions were made to nationalism and to religious groups. Nationalism was still deeply rooted among the Great Russians, the Ukrainians, the nearly 20 million Turkish-speaking people of the Union, and many smaller groups. Concessions to nationalism seemed to fit the position Stalin had adopted two decades previously on the question of nationality; they meant a relaxation of the policy of Russification that the communist regime had inherited from czarism, which was pursued under the name of Sovietization. Concessions to religion were aimed at gaining the support of the sections of the adult population that had never accepted the official atheism of the Soviet regime, and of the religiously-inclined members of the younger generation. It was reckoned at the time that believers, mostly Christians and smaller groups of Moslems and Jews, formed at least one fifth of the adult population. The Orthodox church not only was no longer persecuted, it even was encouraged to absorb other Christian bodies, particularly the Uniats. After a twenty-year lapse, in 1944 the Moslems of the USSR were allowed to resume pilgrimages to Mecca. More important, in order to allay the suspicions of noncommunists, it was decided to dissolve the Comintern (May 1943). The official interpretation of this act was that now every national communist party was on its own, and that there could no longer be any suspicion of "orders from Moscow." Many thought, instead, that the Comintern had simply gone underground.

Under different names, national fronts were organized in most parts of occupied Europe and engaged in sabotage and guerrilla warfare. In France the communists collaborated with General de Gaulle, with democratic socialists, with the Catholics, and with the radicals. They were the animating spirit in the French Council of Resistance. In Italy they were active in promoting the Committee of National Liberation (CLN) in which all political tendencies opposed to fascism were represented. In Greece the communists had received 100,000 votes in 1938, a short time before their party was outlawed by General Metaxas; they now promoted the formation of the National Liberation Front (EAM) which included communists, agrarians, democrats, democratic radicals, and for a short time, socialists. In Yugoslavia, under the leadership of Tito (Josip Broz, 1892–   ) the AVNO (Anti-Fascist Council of National Liberation) was formed, with communists, socialists, agrarians, Catholics, radicals, and democrats represented. Toward the end of the war a Fatherland Front was formed in Bulgaria. It included, besides communists, socialists, agrarians, the nationalist Zveno group, and others. Another Fatherland Front was organized in Albania. In Poland a National Front was formed, inspired by the few Polish communist leaders residing in Moscow who had survived the purges. However, collaboration of all antinazi forces proved to be impossible here because of the deep hatred the Polish nationalistic underground felt for the Soviet Union because of its participation in the downfall of Poland in September 1939, the massacres of Polish prisoners of war, and the deportation of the Polish minority from Soviet-occupied areas.

Where noncommunist antifascist groups refused to collaborate with the communists, new groups with the same name, but led by communist sympathizers, were organized. At times civil war broke out between communists and anticommunist opponents of Germany and fascism. This happened, for instance, in Yugoslavia, where Serbian nationalists under General Mihailovitch were accused of fighting against Tito rather than against the Germans; in Greece, where the EAM was opposed by the guerrillas organized by General Zervas and Colonel Grivas; in Poland, where the large underground which recognized the authority of the government-in-exile in London was subjected to the attacks of the communists, who refused to cooperate in the Warsaw rising of August-September 1944 led by General Komorowsky (Bor). In other countries (France, Italy, Belgium, Norway, Holland, Denmark, Czechoslovakia), the tension between communists and anticommunists within the resistance movement was generally kept under control, thus sparing, at least to some extent, the additional sufferings caused elsewhere by inter-resistance fighting.

Thanks to better cohesion, better discipline, and more experience in underground organization and guerrilla warfare, the communist parties acquired a dominant position in most resistance movements, although their numbers were often smaller than those of the noncommunist underground and guerrilla fighters. They were instrumental in preventing the consolidation of German rule in occupied Europe, besides giving valuable military help to the Allies fighting in Italy, and, later, on the western front. During the resistance period, European communists strengthened their parties, acquired a military organization in many countries, and found themselves in possession of large stocks of arms and ammunition, partly taken from the enemy, partly sent to them by the Western Allies. Their willingness to cooperate with noncommunists, their energy, the moderation of the political, economic, and social programs they put forth during this period, and the prestige of the Soviet Union combined with the state of chaos and confusion in most of continental

Europe at the war's end, enabled the communists to widen the base of their popular support considerably.

In the Western Hemisphere, communists redoubled their activities. In several countries they were strengthened by the arrival of communist refugees from Europe. Everywhere, except possibly in Argentina, they profited by the admiration many felt for the endurance and strength of the Soviet peoples. In the United States and Canada a determined attempt was made, in many instances under the guidance of Soviet representatives, to infiltrate the various branches of the public administration, the military forces, labor unions, and youth organizations. The small communist groups that had for some time existed in Latin American countries enjoyed a freedom of action hitherto unknown. In Mexico, Cuba, Chile, and Brazil they were able to build or take over political and labor organizations. In every country of the Western Hemisphere, the communists were sponsoring causes that appealed to the liberal, radical, and progressive elements of the population: the end of racial and religious discrimination, the spread of education, social legislation, government intervention in economic affairs to correct the abuses of capitalism, and the like. Fascism was the only enemy, and antidemocratic slogans were dropped.

During this period, communism appeared to many to be just another political movement, willing to play according to the rules of parliamentary democracies. Why consider it differently from other parties?

In the Far East, nominal collaboration was established between nationalists and communists in China, although the communists rejected the fusion of armed forces that could have guaranteed the unification of Chinese political forces. In Korea, Indo-China, Burma, in the Philippine Islands, Malaya, Indonesia, in short, in all countries occupied by the Japanese, communist organizers tried to imitate what their colleagues had achieved in most of Europe. Their success was less spectacular, but by the time the war came to an end they had nuclei strong enough to influence the political changes that were occurring.

In China, since the revolution of 1911, there had been an almost uninterrupted succession of internal and external conflicts, and when the war ended the Chinese nation was exhausted. The pressure of the West had caused a landslide involving every aspect of Chinese life, thought, and religion, as well as economics and politics. The institutions inherited from the past centuries, and the traditional values on which they had been based, had weakened. The relationship between individuals and classes that had made sense in what had been a paternalistic authoritarian society, had now become meaningless. A deep economic transformation was taking place. A wretched and unstable urban proletariat filled the new industrial cities, which had sprung up along the coast and in the northeastern provinces; contacts with a new wealthy class made the peasants increasingly aware of their own poverty. The family, the village community, and traditional education were no longer able to keep their hold.

In other areas of the Far East, the situation was not very different from what prevailed in China proper. Korea and Manchuria had been *de facto* Japanese colonies. The defeat of the Japanese left a political vacuum that no local force was able to fill. On the mainland and in the islands of southeastern Asia, the Japanese invasion had dealt a severe blow to British, French, and Dutch colonial administrations. The political and economic structures built by Europeans in the course of generations were swept away

during the three and a half years of Japanese control.
Chaos and disorder reigned. From Java to Manchuria
the situation in 1945 was not unlike that which developed in Russia in 1917 after the collapse of the
czarist regime. Here was a chance for a small but
militant and aggressive group to seize control. It
would have been against the theory and practice of
communism to let the golden opportunity pass.

The Postwar Expansion of Communism: Communist-controlled Areas (1945-1952)

The end of World War II in Europe (May 1945)
found much of the Continent in a state of anarchy.
Fascist rule had been the equivalent of a revolution.
Millions of people had been killed, tens of millions
uprooted; for years, suffering had been part and parcel
of life. Political and economic institutions had collapsed. Beliefs, values, ideas around which the social
structure of many European nations had been organized, had either disappeared or their influence had
lessened considerably. Nazi-fascism had suffered a
crushing military defeat; there were still plenty of
individual fascists, but they were isolated units and
hence incapable of action. Conservatism and capitalism
as organized social forces were weakened by the fall
of fascism. Liberalism had withered to an extent un-
thinkable a generation earlier. Liberal parties, whether
of the right or the left, were only a faint reflection of
what they had been. The liberal animus had largely
vanished and the liberals' sense of justice and aspiration toward equality, which make liberty meaningful,
had declined. Because of this, attachment to what
used to be liberal institutions had become an expression of conservatism. Democratic socialism was still

numerically important but its inability to check the advance of authoritarianism in the previous twenty years had exposed its fundamental lack of energy. This lack was largely the result of the conflict, not yet resolved by socialists, between (a) the desire to establish collectivism, which requires an authoritarian framework, and (b) a genuine attachment to liberty, which requires at least some degree of autonomy in the pursuit of economic activities. Nationalism was still a powerful emotion, if less so than in the recent past, but had little organization in the form of parties. In nations predominantly Catholic or Orthodox, the postwar political vacuum was only partially filled by several varieties of Christian socialism or Christian democracy. Under conditions of disorder, poverty, confusion, deluded hopes, and intense hatreds, communism found an atmosphere conducive to its further development.

From a communist viewpoint, the most important result of the war was the strengthening of the Soviet Union. In May 1945 Soviet troops were in total occupation of what, before 1938, had been eight independent states in Europe: Estonia, Latvia, Lithuania, Poland, Czechoslovakia, Hungary, Rumania and Bulgaria. Parts of Germany, Austria, Finland, Norway, and the Danish island of Bornholm were also occupied by forces of the USSR. In addition some Soviet troops were stationed in Yugoslavia and Albania, where power was firmly held by the communist leaders Tito and Hodja (or Hoxha, 1908–   ).

Soviet troops were soon withdrawn from northern Norway and Bornholm. The annexations of 1939 and 1940 were confirmed through agreements among the big powers that were reached at Teheran, Yalta, and Potsdam. To them were added sections of northeastern Germany and southeastern Czechoslovakia. This represented a total of about 185,000 square miles with over 23 million inhabitants, of which about 40,000 square miles with nearly 8 million inhabitants had never belonged to imperial Russia. In the Far East, no one objected to the formal annexation in 1944 of the former Chinese territory of Tannu Tuva, *de facto* a Soviet area since 1921. Manchuria, Korea north of the 38th parallel, southern Sakhalin, and the Kurile islands were occupied by the Soviets, who annexed the two last-named territories (about 20,000 square miles and 500,000 inhabitants). A Soviet-supported regime ruled Mongolia. The wealth of the annexed territories largely compensated for the economic losses the Soviet Union suffered in the war.

During the war there had been considerable talk among people who did not understand the dynamics of the communist movement about a possible "liberalization" of the Soviet regime—in the sense of allowing some intellectual and political freedom—and about the concession of real self-government to the sixteen republics of the Union. There had been mention of differences between the communist party, the bureaucracy, and the armed forces, of tension between the ruling oligarchy and the new middle class of managers and professional people, (accounting for 9 or 10 percent of the population), of dissensions within the higher levels of the communist oligarchy, of a desire for freedom of expression among the intelligentsia. The fact that out of several million prisoners of war possibly as many as 200,000 Ukrainians and 80,000 Moslems from the Caucasus and Soviet Central Asia had agreed to fight for the Germans had been interpreted to mean that the Soviet Union's cohesiveness was not as great as had been supposed in the late 1930s.

With the war's end, however, there was no indication that the internal solidity of the Soviet Union had declined or that the authority of its leaders was challenged. Not everyone in the Union was happy about the development of socialism. The official line nevertheless remained the nation's line and the masses confidently expected the realization of their leaders' promise that standards of living would soon equal those of the Americans. Seven ethnic groups were deprived of what the Soviets call national and cultural autonomy, because of the sympathy which a majority of their people had shown towards the German invaders. Measures were taken in 1946 to stamp out what appeared to be a recrudescence of nationalism in the Ukraine. When elections took place, the customary plebiscite went to the candidates chosen by the communist organizations.

After 1945 the backing of the Soviet Union was, even more than before 1939, instrumental in guaranteeing the influence of communist parties in every corner of the globe. It is reckoned that the Soviet Union lost over 7 million dead in the war against Germany and spent on the war effort, at the official rate of exchange, nearly $200 billion (corresponding in real value to approximately $60–80 billion). In spite of these losses, the Soviet Union was stronger than ever. Internationally, the Soviet Union enjoyed a better position than Russia had ever had. In 1914 there had been seven great powers in the Eastern Hemisphere; in 1945, besides the Soviet Union, only one remained—a considerably weakened United Kingdom. Militant communism was encouraged by the first postwar five-year plan, with an emphasis on heavy industry that could be interpreted as a willingness to use violent methods if peaceful ones failed.

In Europe, Soviet military occupation was the prelude to the establishment of communist dictatorships.

European states not annexed by the Soviet Union but included at the end of the war in the Soviet sphere of influence (Albania, Bulgaria, Czechoslovakia, Hungary, Poland, Rumania), and the Soviet zone of Germany (later the German Democratic Republic), cover an area of about 400,000 square miles and have a population of over 100 million, with total national incomes equivalent to nearly one third of the official national income of the Soviet Union. Since 1945 they have been referred to as the satellites.[7] Postwar developments in these countries followed a similar pattern, as they also did in communist but not Soviet-controlled Yugoslavia.

When, as the result of Soviet military victories, the Germans were compelled to evacuate or surrender, the victorious Russians or their allies (such as the Yugoslav partisans) put power in the hands of a coalition government composed of representatives of the groups that had participated in the antinazi national fronts during the war. The main feature of these coalition governments was the appointment of a communist as minister of the interior who, in European countries, has direct control over the police. Noncoalition parties, on the pretext—sometimes untrue, as in the case of Poland—that they had aided and abetted fascism, were outlawed or prevented from exercising any influence by being deprived of using means of communication (press, radio, cars, meeting places, and so forth), all strictly controlled by the government. At the same time a fairly considerable section of the economy was nationalized in order to make producers more dependent on the government.

Having acquired full control of the police, the com-

[7] Isolated from the satellites as a result of the break between the Soviet Union and Yugoslavia in 1948, and of the communist defeat in Greece in 1949, Albania pursued an autonomous course after 1958.

munists proceeded to the second phase: the weakening, through arrests and threats, of noncommunist members of the coalition who showed signs of independence. In the Soviet-controlled countries and Yugoslavia this phase occupied most of 1946 and part of 1947.

The third phase was characterized by the structural reorganization of the state and the consolidation of communist political monopoly. The appearances of the coalitions were usually kept up, with a few well-chosen cryptocommunists (such as Cyrankiewicz in Poland, Dinnyes in Hungary, Fierlinger in Czechoslovakia) representing noncommunist groups. All organized opposition was liquidated. Fundamental liberties (personal liberty, freedom of expression, of conscience, of teaching, of association, of movement, among others) were abolished or restricted to the point of suppression. Rapid advances were made in collectivization, transforming most citizens into wage or salary earners whose livelihood was dependent on the government. State monopoly was established over education, the press, and all other means of communication. Forced-labor camps were opened or expanded. Recalcitrant or potentially recalcitrant citizens were arrested. A few were sentenced to death and shot or hanged in order to intimidate those who still harbored resentment against the communist dictatorship. This final phase was reached in Albania, Bulgaria, Rumania, and Yugoslavia by the end of 1947. Poland, Czechoslovakia, and Hungary reached it in 1948, Eastern Germany in 1949.

A fourth phase was a purely internal communist affair. It corresponded to Stalin's purges and concerned the elimination of actual or potential opposition to the dominant faction within the communist parties. It began in 1948 and ended in 1952. Only a few hundred people were executed, but this was enough to inspire the fear that acts as a prime deterrent of oppositional activities. By the end of 1952 each party seemed, on the surface, to have achieved the monolithic unity that is a basic Leninist principle. (Later events would show that such party unity had not yet been realized in Poland and Hungary).

The speed of the communist advance was partly regulated by internal conditions. In Czechoslovakia there was a relatively high standard of living and education, lively nationalism and, in large sections of the population, fairly strong democratic feeling. In East Germany strong nationalism remained, but twelve years of ruthless nazi repression had weakened all democratic forces to the point of near extinction. In the other countries there was little democratic strength or tradition. Poland and Hungary had been ruled, in the period between the two wars, by the corrupt and weak descendants of what had once been a virile and responsible feudal class; Bulgaria, Rumania, Yugoslavia and Albania by despots who had little root among the peasant population of their countries. Once the old political structure had been swept away, the only political force that could have checked the advance of communism was agrarian socialism. This was represented in Poland by the Polish Peasant party led by Mikolajczyk, in Hungary by the Smallholders party under ineffectual leadership, in Rumania by the followers of Maniu; in Yugoslavia by those of Macek, and in Bulgaria by the movement led by D. Dimitrov and N. Petkov. Agrarian socialism had numbers but lacked organization. The communists were efficiently organized and were helped by the presence of Soviet troops. The struggle could hardly be called such, as agrarian socialism was nowhere able to put up serious opposition. It collapsed as easily in these countries in 1945–1947 as its Russian counterpart, the Socialist Revolutionary party, had done in 1918–1919.

In four countries, either a majority (as in Poland, Czechoslovakia, and Hungary) or a large minority (in Yugoslavia) of the people had been reared in the beliefs and institutions of Roman Catholicism. In these countries the Catholic Church was the only organization that seriously tried to put up a certain amount of resistance. But it fought a rapidly losing battle. The arrest and trial of a few members of the hierarchy (cardinals, archbishops, and bishops) was enough to intimidate a good many of the clergy. Through the nationalization of wealth, the clergy were reduced to the servile position of all bureaucrats in authoritarian regimes. Their cohesion was weakened by the presence of a few procommunist clerics. By the end of 1952 it seemed as though Catholicism in Soviet-controlled Europe (with the possible exception of Poland) might soon lose all political, maybe also intellectual, significance. Other religious bodies (Orthodox Christians in Rumania, Bulgaria and Yugoslavia; the Protestant minority in Hungary; the Moslems in Albania and Yugoslavia) offered even less resistance than the Catholic Church, and accepted, on the whole, the position of obedient cogs in the new dictatorial machinery.

Events in the Soviet zone of Germany followed a somewhat similar pattern. At first, as in other zones, four political parties had been authorized by the victors: Social Democratic, Christian Socialist, Communist, and Liberal Democratic. Taking advantage of the usual socialist split between those who gave priority to democracy and those who gave priority to collectivism, the Soviet authorities were able to bring about a fusion of the latter with the communists, under W. Pieck (1876–1960) and W. Ulbricht (1883–   ).

This led to the establishment of the Unified Socialist
party. The Social Democratic party, which anticommunist socialists would have liked to organize, was
outlawed. At the end of 1947, J. Kaiser and other
Christian socialists were forced to abandon the leadership of the Christian socialists and were replaced with
procommunists. Liberal democrats, unwilling to accept
communist orders, were compelled to find refuge in
the Western zones of Germany. Whatever the appearances, four and a half years after the end of the war,
East Germany was solidly in the grip of the communists.
Just as under the nazi regime non-nazis had faced
the choice of being liquidated sooner or later, or acting
as nazis, so under the new rule most citizens, whatever their secret thoughts and aspirations, decided to
conform. In the course of the years, until 1961, several
millions abandoned their homes and escaped to West
Germany.

The close relationship between all these countries
and the Soviet Union was made clear in June-July
1947, when they were compelled to reject the invitation sent by the British and French governments to
participate in a common effort for the economic
recovery of Europe through the Marshall Plan. Under
the leadership of the Soviet Union, steps were taken
toward economic integration of communist-controlled
states through a system of trade agreements (then
called the Molotov Plan). The agreements aimed at
increasing economic exchanges between the various
states, at reducing their dependence on Western capital and markets, and at achieving a considerable
amount of industrialization through their own resources. The Molotov Plan took concrete shape in
the Mutual Assistance Organization (Comecon) consisting, since 1961, of the Soviet Union, six European
satellites, and Mongolia.

What the Molotov Plan was supposed to achieve on an economic level the Cominform aimed to realize on intellectual and political levels. The central control established by Stalin's group in the 1920s over the communist movement, as a whole, had weakened during World War II. This weakening could easily lead to the development of heresies, or "deviations," in the communist parties outside the Soviet Union. To maintain orthodoxy and conformity, central power had to be institutionalized, and at the same time supplied with the means to enforce its control. This led to the establishment (September 1947) of the *Cominform* (Communist Information Bureau), organized at a meeting held in Poland, in which the leaders of eight European parties, including those of Italy and France, participated. As had been the case nearly thirty years earlier, the communist leadership felt that greater cohesion and coercion were needed for the successful achievement of communist aims and aspirations.

It is probable that when the Cominform was established, the Soviet authorities already had misgivings about Tito, the leader of Yugoslav communists. For over a quarter of a century he had been a loyal party official. The accidents of war had made him a leader strong in his own right. The withdrawal and surrender of the Germans had left him in complete control of Yugoslavia—a country lying on the western border of the Soviet sphere of influence, and thus enjoying the possibility of direct relations with the Western powers. Moreover, Yugoslavia was endowed with natural defenses and considerable resources. Distrust of Tito led the other members of the Cominform to accept the Yugoslav capital, Belgrade, as the headquarters of the organization—the best place from which to keep an eye on a potential rebel. We do not yet know the exact reasons leading to the rupture between Tito and the Cominform in 1948 when, in view of the forthcoming struggle with the Western powers, greater discipline was demanded of all communists. It is possible that Tito rejected Soviet plans for the rapid collectivization of the Yugoslav economy. Or perhaps he wanted to launch an attack against Greece, or Italy, or Austria, and the Soviet leaders did not yet want to become involved in a major conflict. Perhaps the realization of a Balkan federation (desired by Tito) would have led Balkan communism into the paths of revisionism, or even of socialist agrarianism, hated by the Soviet leaders because of its democratic features. Or again, there may have been nothing but a clash of strong personalities.

Whatever the reason, in 1948 the break occurred. Tito and his advisers (among whom the foremost were Pijade and Kardelj) found it necessary to formulate a communist ideology different from Soviet ideology. Stalinist communism was based on the twin concepts of total centralization and power from above. Yugoslav communists, in self-defense, began to stress the concepts of decentralization and power from below, thus moving one step towards the fundamental Western democratic concept of the individual's autonomy and responsibility. Decentralization and power from below meant, politically, rendering Yugoslav federalism effective; economically it meant replacing a hierarchically organized economy with considerable autonomy and responsibility in the hands of local bodies and workers' organizations.

Hopes connected with a large-scale development of Titoist nationalist and federalist communism were high among noncommunists in 1948 and the following years. The American government subsidized Tito to the tune of over $3 billion in a period of fifteen years to give him the possibility of resisting Soviet threats and blandishments. Results, however, fell considerably short of hopes. The effect of Titoism on the communist movement outside Yugoslavia was slight. A few purges were enough to deter would-be imitators. Communists need clear, rational formulations of their positions; the Yugoslav leaders either lacked the intellectual capacity or—more likely—the will to engage in the kind of effort once made by Lenin and later by Stalin and Mao. In any case, there was no cogent formulation, and Titoist national-communism remained an expression without clear ideological content.

As long as Stalin lived, the mutual hatred he and Tito felt for each other was a deciding factor in the making of Yugoslav policy. After Stalin's death and for several years thereafter, the deciding factor for Yugoslav communists was a desire for national independence, and for Tito the ambition to play an autonomous role in world affairs. In 1954 the attempt to formulate a schismatic communist ideology was abandoned. During 1955–1961 Tito tried hard to set himself up as a major leader of so-called uncommitted nations. In so doing he acted as a nationalist, not as a communist. Within communism, Titoism had less of an impact than Trotskyism had had in the twenties and thirties, or Maoism in the late fifties and in the sixties.

In Asia, the Soviet attempt in the immediate postwar period to create a system of buffer states controlled by local communist groups, either kept in hand by Russian leadership or simply affiliated with Soviet communism, met with varying success. It failed in the west (in Turkey, Iran, and the Arab nations—see next section), and succeeded in the east.

Afghanistan and what used to be called outlying regions of China (such as Sinkiang, Mongolia, Man-

churia) border on the Soviet Union. No attempt was
made by Soviet representatives to stimulate the growth
of a communist organization in Afghanistan. Long-
range considerations of foreign policy prevailed over
immediate party interests. An excess of communist
activities would have disturbed the good relations
that had existed since 1919 between Afghanistan, who
served as a watchdog over both Iran and the Indian
subcontinent, and the Soviet Union. Furthermore, according to the Marxist-Leninist historical scheme, the
traditional authoritarian regime of Afghanistan was
more acceptable to communists than a democratic
or socialdemocratic regime.

Farther east, in Sinkiang, the largest and westernmost province of China, the USSR had exercised a
good deal of influence over local tribes during the
greater part of the 1930s. There was a withdrawal
during World War II, when Soviet leaders sought to
inspire confidence in the members of the nationalist
government which, at that time, ruled most of nonoc-
cupied China and was bent on fighting Germany's
ally in the Far East, Japan. At the end of 1947 Soviet
influence was reestablished through the support of
anti-Chinese tribes whose kinsmen lived in Soviet central Asia. After the proclamation of the People's
Republic in China, Soviet officials and troops withdrew from Sinkiang, which came under direct Chinese
communist control. Still farther east, Mongolia,
closely linked to the Soviet Union since 1921, remained
within the Soviet sphere of influence and was in reality
as much a part of the Soviet Union as the five Soviet
republics of central Asia. Most of Manchuria had
been occupied by Soviet troops in 1945; their subse-
quent withdrawal was effectuated so as to leave the
country and its considerable resources in the hands
of Chinese communists.

As the result of an agreement between the American and the Soviet governments at the end of the war, Soviet troops occupied Korea north of the 38th parallel, a territory of about 50,000 square miles with a population of around 9 million. Under the supervision of Soviet agents and led by Kim Il-sung, Korean communists acted as their colleagues in the European satellite countries had done. Opponents and potential opponents were destroyed. Power was concentrated in the hands of the hierarchically organized communist party. State monopoly was imposed over means of communication and education. Much of the wealth was nationalized. A few reforms were introduced in order to give the inhabitants the impression that from now on they would be properly looked after by the state. A People's Republic was proclaimed in 1948; immediately, with feverish activity and good results, a relatively large army of probably not less than 200,000 men in fighting units was organized, commanded by Soviet officers and by Koreans who had been trained militarily either by the Japanese or by the Chinese communists.

Encouraged by an American statement in January 1950 that seemed to exclude Korea from the American line of defense, the communist government of North Korea attacked South Korea on June 25, 1950. The Korean war soon became, whatever its appearances, a war between the United States and China. During one year of major fighting and nearly two years of minor fighting, it brought untold suffering to the Korean people. The war had far-reaching effects as well. At the time it convinced the American nation that force was an important factor in communist expansion and that force had to be checked by force. It was a major factor, at the end of 1952, in the formulation of Stalin's policy—since followed by

Soviet communists—of avoiding a military clash with the United States while maintaining all-out aggressiveness. The Korean war strengthened internal unity in China, and for three years weakened the pressure of Chinese communism on southeast Asia and of Soviet communism on western Europe and the Middle East.

By far the most important event in the immediate postwar period was the victory of the Chinese communists and the establishment of a communist state in the "closed continent," the home of the oldest great civilization still in existence. As in the case of eastern Europe, the communist success in China was due mainly to the intelligent use of violence by a strongly integrated and highly cohesive minority group endowed with a fanatical belief in the righteousness of its cause. To this factor, inherent in the communist movement, must be added others that had nothing to do with the Chinese communists. The Japanese aggression had dislocated China, exhausted large sections of the population, and had prevented the nationalists from concentrating all their efforts on unifying the country. The occupation of Manchuria by Soviet troops made possible the transfer to the Chinese communists, at a critical moment, of large stocks of Japanese arms and ammunition. Partly because of unwillingness and partly because of inefficiency, the nationalist regime failed to carry out a badly needed agrarian reform and to maintain law and order—which were sadly lacking in many areas under their control.

The pressure exercised by the United States Government over the nationalists to induce them to collaborate with the communists was another element that should not be ignored or minimized. This pressure was based on the assumption, stressed by numerous writers on Far Eastern affairs, of a fundamental difference between Russian and Chinese communism. Chinese communist leaders had always held that they were Marxist-Leninist. The faction in power since 1932 had conducted itself loyally according to the Stalinist line. But American experts insisted that Chinese communism was not Leninist, and even less Stalinist, but extreme agrarian reformism. In the state of chaos in which China found itself, power was bound to fall into the hands of the best organized minority. Only foreign intervention could have kept in power a divided and inefficient minority such as that represented by the Kuomintang.

Throughout the war against Japan, which lasted, with brief intervals of peace, for fourteen years (1931–1945), relations between nationalists and communists in China had remained strained in spite of several attempts at collaboration. During the last stages of the war, the nationalists had insisted on unification of the armed forces as the price for eventual collaboration in the government with the communists. While the war was in progress, the communists were concerned about building up their own strength and had no intention of giving up what they knew to be the most important element in the struggle for final success. In the summer of 1945, the communists had about 1 million men under arms and were in control of large areas in northern China. Their guerrillas took over districts evacuated by the Japanese in the eastern provinces before the nationalists had time to arrive.

The occupation of Manchuria by Soviet troops in August 1945 influenced the course of events more than anything else. A considerable economic expansion had been effected by the Japanese in Manchuria, severed from China in 1931 and *de facto* independent even before then. In August 1945, a treaty had been rashly signed between the Chinese government (which

was under the impression that it was implementing
American policies) and the Soviet government. The
treaty recognized on the one hand the end of Chinese
sovereignty over Outer Mongolia and limited Soviet
rights in Manchuria and, on the other, it recognized
Chinese sovereignty over Manchuria. When the Soviet
troops withdrew, most of the vacated areas were
handed over to the communists. Two years after V–J
Day, the communist forces numbered 2 million well-
trained and well-equipped men.

Fighting between nationalists and communists
varied in intensity, but never stopped entirely. At
first there were nationalist offensives, such as the one
that led to their temporary occupation of Yenan
(March 1947), the capital of the communist area. When
fresh and newly equipped communist divisions took
the offensive, the nationalist military leaders made
the strategic blunder of trying to hold Manchuria, a
region far from China proper. Their best troops were
encircled and compelled to surrender. Defeat followed
defeat, peasant dissatisfaction led to a general anti-
nationalist *jacquerie,* and by the end of 1949 the whole
of mainland China was in the hands of the communists.
A People's Republic had been proclaimed on September 21, with its capital at Peiping. Under nationalist
control remained the island of Formosa—technically,
until the signing of the peace treaty with Japan in
1951, a Japanese possession, and then the refuge of
the nationalist government. Besides a few smaller
islands, Hainan, southwest of Formosa, was held for
a while by nationalist forces.

Following the example set by the states of Eastern
Europe, communist China had a nominal coalition
government. In reality it was a one-party police state
run by the highly centralized and hierarchically or-

ganized Communist party. No opposition or dissent was tolerated. Class liquidation was carried out as efficiently as in the Soviet Union thirty years before. All media of communication were strictly controlled by the government. Parts of the economy were nationalized immediately; the rest was rigidly controlled by the government, which held the monopoly of economic initiative. It was reported that in 1950 executions of so-called counterrevolutionaries had claimed nearly 1 million victims. In Marxist-Leninist jargon the people executed were either monopolists (businessmen and landlords) or lackeys of imperialism (democrats). In 1951 the liquidation of counterrevolutionaries continued. Early in the year Tibet was occupied. All educational, cultural, charitable, and religious foreign institutions were nationalized; all Chinese Christian churches were ordered to sever relations with foreign missions. The following year saw the end of all organized opposition, the intensive "reeducation" of pro-Western intellectuals, and the establishment of a complete network of state trusts, trading corporations, and cooperatives for the control of all aspects of the economy. Extensive economic agreements with the Soviet Union accompanied the launching, early in 1953, of the first five-year plan.

Although the masses in China cared little for communism or anticommunism (and had no voice or possibility of expressing their views), communism appealed to a larger minority of the population than democracy ever had. The concept of liberty and the accompanying value of individual responsibility and dignity were never strong in the Chinese tradition; traditional Chinese society had possessed an excellent system for the control of the human mind and had developed political despotism to a fine art. The communist regime took over where China had left off in 1842, adding economic control to political and intellectual control.

By the end of 1949, the communist movement, which fifty years before was only an idea in the minds of a few hundred or a few thousand radicals, had achieved complete power over one fourth of the land area of the globe (excluding the Antarctic), inhabited by one third of the world's population. The extraordinary success of communism in just a few years could be compared to the Roman conquest of the Mediterranean in the second century B.C., to the Islamic expansion of the seventh century, to the empires conquered in a few years by Attila, Genghis Khan, and Timur.

Postwar Communism outside Communist-controlled areas (1945-1952)

Until the last year of the Stalinist era, control over as many as possible of the advanced industrial nations of continental Europe and the disruption of those which could not be controlled remained major communist goals. The priority given to the communization of industrial Europe had been inherited from nineteenth-century socialism and from Leninism. There was, however, growing resistance west of the Iron Curtain [8] against internal and external communist pressures—at least partly as a result of American aid and the stiffening of American anticommunism. Because of this, a major change in communist global

[8] The expression "Iron Curtain" was used by Winston Churchill in his speech at Independence, Missouri, of March 1946; it came to indicate the European boundaries of Soviet-controlled areas.

tactics was decided on by Stalin and his collaborators in 1952. The change was not less important than the changes in 1923 (tactical retreat outside the Soviet Union), 1927 (aloofness), 1934 (popular fronts), 1939 (communist-fascist common front against democracy), 1945 (all-out opposition to the United States). Free Europe would no longer have priority in communist efforts to seize power. This priority would be transferred to the underdeveloped areas. Communist efforts should aim at isolating western Europe and the United States from the rest of the world, at stimulating internal tensions, at strengthening anti-Americanism everywhere.

In the immediate postwar years, the greatest communist successes were achieved in France and Italy. This was partly the result of the excellent organization built up by the communists during the period of German occupation and of their activity in the resistance movements of those countries. In the first postwar French elections held in 1945, the Communist party, which used to receive about one vote in seven before World War II, improved its position considerably and obtained the support of more than one fourth of the voters. Party members numbered nearly 1 million. During the following years its voting strength increased to 29 percent; in the elections of 1951 it still drew more than 25 percent of the vote, in spite of economic recovery and the reorganization of anticommunist forces. In the 1951 parliament the communists formed the second largest group. For nearly three years after the liberation of the country they participated in coalition governments, except for the short-lived government led by the socialist Léon Blum (December 17, 1946–January 22, 1947). In May 1947 the socialists—accusing the communists of sabotaging the efforts of the government from the

inside and of making use of their position to strengthen
their own party, and supported by the Catholics of
the *Mouvement Républicain Populaire* and by the
liberals of the Radical Socialist Party—decided to form
a government without communist participation. Later
in the year an anticommunist rightist movement was
organized by General de Gaulle. It received a plurality
of votes in the municipal elections of 1947, and in
1951 sent to the parliament the largest single bloc
of deputies. From then on communist influence declined, although a large minority of the French remained loyal to Marxism-Leninism.

In Italy, communist ministers sat in coalition governments April 1944–May 1947. At the general elections of June 2, 1946, the first free elections since 1921,
the communists received just under one fifth of the
votes. Under the leadership of Togliatti, the Italian
Communist party then became the largest outside the
communist empire with a membership that already
totaled more than 2 million. In May 1947, the leader
of the Christian democrats resigned as premier and,
entrusted with the formation of a new cabinet, formed
a homogeneous one of Christian democrats and in-
dependents. This was strengthened at the end of the
year by the inclusion of representatives of small democratic groups. Contrary to what was happening in
France, a majority of Italian socialists decided in
favor of close collaboration with the Communist party,
from which they became almost indistinguishable.
The collaboration lasted until the events of 1956–
1957. At the national elections of April 1948, and
again at the local elections of 1951, communists and
socialists voted together. It is supposed that the strictly
communist vote increased by about 50 percent, from
4 to 6 million voters. In the parliament the communists
formed the second largest group. "Deviation" was

kept firmly under control. Some intellectuals left the party and a few deputies were expelled. This caused a number of speculations concerning "Titoism," but only a negligible influence was exercised at first by the dissidents over the masses of the faithful. In April 1951 the party leadership announced a total membership of over 2½ million.

The collapse of nazism had brought about a limited revival of the communist movement in the non-Soviet zones of Germany, where more than seven tenths of the German people lived. In 1932 the Communist party had been the third largest, ranking after the nazis and the social-democrats. After the defeat of 1945 the communists were competing with the Christian democrats, the social-democrats, and the liberals. Under conditions of freedom of vote guaranteed by the occupying forces of the United States, Great Britain, and France, the communists could nowhere obtain more than a small fraction of the vote. In the *länder* of the three zones, the largest percentage of votes was received by the Christian democrats in predominantly Catholic areas, elsewhere by the social-democrats. The communists made a determined effort to forge ahead, but with remarkably little success. They were able to recruit less than 200,000 members and at the first postwar elections in 1949, polled a little over 1 million votes. The local elections of 1952 showed that they had lost ground, and that their voting strength was not more than 2–4 percent of the electorate, according to the *länder*.

In the Austrian general elections that took place in 1949 and again in 1953, the communists received less than one vote in twenty. The prestige of the small Austrian Communist party was at first strengthened by the presence of the Soviet army of occupation. This prestige later declined almost to vanishing point.

In the Scandinavian countries, in Holland, Belgium, and Luxemburg, communist parties at first improved their position in comparison with the prewar period. But they soon lost what extra influence they had gained, and remained small and relatively unimportant. Political leadership was retained in the hands of social-democrats and liberals in Scandinavia, of Christian democrats in the Benelux countries. In Finland and Iceland, the communists were proportionately more numerous but failed to gain the upper hand. In Switzerland and in the British Isles as well, the communists remained small noisy minorities with little weight in political affairs. In Spain and Portugal they existed then only as small underground groups.

In Greece there had been little or no evidence of communist participation in the war between Greece and the Axis (October 1940–April 1941). After the nazi attack on the Soviet Union, the communists, together with other groups, took active part in the resistance. After the withdrawal of the Germans in October 1944, they attempted to overthrow the Greek coalition government of which they had been members. The revolt was put down by the combined efforts of British troops and Greek anticommunist forces. The communists and various procommunist groups refused to participate in the elections of March 31, 1946. Allied observers—British, American, and French —expressed the opinion that, had the communists participated in the elections, they and the fellow-travelers would have received less than one third of the votes. They decided instead on guerrilla activities, favored by the mountainous nature of the country and by its extensive frontier with Bulgaria, Yugoslavia, and Albania, all controlled by communists. By the end of 1946, considerable guerrilla activity had been carried out under the military leadership of Markos

Vafiades (1906– ?). During 1947, attacks were made against many towns and villages in the northern provinces. A commission sent by the United Nations to investigate the situation reported that the communist-led guerrillas, then estimated at 15,000 men, were receiving help from the communist dictatorships of Bulgaria, Yugoslavia, and Albania.

The deterioration of the situation in Greece and the possibility that the conflict between communists and anticommunists would lead to further complications and to the establishment of a communist regime caused the United States Government, in March 1947, to take a direct interest in the internal affairs of the country. The Communist party was outlawed. At the end of December 1947 a provisional government was formed by the communists in the area of Mount Grammos. The reorganization of the Greek forces under the supervision of American experts and Tito's defection from the Soviet camp contributed toward bringing the civil war to an end early in 1949. At the 1952 general elections only a small section of the population showed itself to be in favor of communism: the cryptocommunist EDA received about 150,000 votes.

As already mentioned, the Soviet attempt to create a system of buffer states controlled by local communists failed in western Asia, that is, Turkey, Iran, and Arab countries. During World War II and periodically after, there were Soviet threats against Turkey. Pressure against Turkey was also exercised through Bulgarians (there were serious frontier incidents) and Soviet Armenians clamoring for Turkish provinces once inhabited by Armenians. As a result of the severe anticommunist policy followed by Turkish nationalists since 1919, there was no organized group in Turkey capable of lending support to the activities of native or foreign communists, and Soviet attempts to intimidate the Turkish republic failed.

During World War II, Soviet troops occupied the northern provinces of Iran, and the British occupied the southwestern section of the country. The Soviet troops were to have left Iran a few months after the end of the hostilities, as the British did, but when the time came they did not move. Combined British-American pressure, exercised through the United Nations, induced the Soviet Government to order the evacuation of Iran in 1946. This was done in such a way as to leave behind in Azerbaijan—the most populous province, inhabited by people akin to those of Soviet Azerbaijan—a communist-controlled provincial administration. A few months later, the central government of Iran sent an expeditionary force and after brief fighting reestablished its authority. Subsequently, waves of nervousness swept Iran each time Soviet troops moved along the border. To this was added, from time to time, the agitation of Kurdish tribesmen, acting under communist influence both in Iran and Iraq. In contrast to what happened in Turkey, a section of the Iranian intelligentsia embraced communism and the Iranian Communist party, in spite of the lack of any sizable mass following, was able to maintain a fairly efficient underground organization.

In general, postwar communist progress was considerably slower in Islamic nations than in other parts of the world. By the time World War II ended there were active, although not large, communist groups only in French North Africa, mostly in Algeria, in some of the states of the Middle East (Syria, Lebanon, Iran), and farther east in Indonesia. Religion was a strong barrier against the spread of communism. Islam is not in itself more anticommunist than Christainity, but on the whole religion probably means more to Moslems than to Christians. Moreover, the influential groups of the population were then either fanatically traditionalist, or (in the case of most of the intelligentsia) fanatically nationalist. In some Arab nations, particularly, the combination of extreme nationalism and vague socialism has produced movements more akin to European fascism than to Soviet communism.

The communist leaders' attempt to create a pro-Soviet attitude in the Moslem countries by allowing Soviet Moslems to travel outside the USSR did not give appreciable results. And in 1947, on the pretext of danger of epidemics, Soviet Moslems were again forbidden to make their pilgrimage to Mecca. In Syria the Communist party was outlawed at the end of 1947. At times, however, some Arab governments flirted with the idea of agreements with the Soviet Union for nationalistic reasons. Since acquiring independence in 1932 Iraq had been governed by a Westernized minority. A few intellectuals called themselves communists; Kurds in the north were, for tribal reasons, open to Soviet overtures; but communism was yet hardly a political factor. The same can be said of Egypt, even before the 1952 revolution that put a nationalist socialist dictatorship in power. There were active communists in Lebanon and among Palestinian Arabs, but few in the other independent or near-independent Arab nations. In Pakistan, a minor communist agitation, which was mainly connected with Indian communism, existed only in the eastern section of the country. In Malaya, communism failed to penetrate the Moslem section of the population.

Only in Indonesia, the most populous Moslem state, did communists have a strong organization before 1952. There, Dutch and Indonesian communists had been active for several decades. They took advantage of the chaotic conditions that followed the end of Japanese occupation and the proclamation of independence by a group of Japanese-sponsored nationalists to strengthen their organization. Attempts at open revolt in October 1949 were crushed by the nationalists; in the fighting the communist leader Muso died, as did also the former leader Tan Malaka. After riots in Jakarta in August 1951, many communists were arrested. Shortly afterwards came a *coup de scène:* nationalists and communists made common cause against the moderates and the socialists. From then on communist influence increased rapidly.

The agitation for independence and the tense situation accompanying and following independence in 1947 provided fertile ground for communist activities in India. Many leaders of the Congress party had been in sympathy with the Soviet Union—just as some of them had favored the Axis during the war—simply because the USSR and the Axis were against Great Britain. Small groups of British-educated Indian intellectuals had been attracted by Marxism-Leninism. For many years, Roy and British-born Palme Dutt had consistently occupied high positions in the counsels of the Comintern. After independence, the communists intensified their efforts, particularly in the southern states of the country, where ethnic problems heightened social tension. At the national elections of 1951–1952, communist candidates received nearly 6 million votes; not a high percentage of the total (about 100 million votes had been cast), but all the same a remarkable success. However, communist agitation was checked at first by measures introduced by the government, which was controlled by the dominant Congress party. In some of the states communist organizations were outlawed. Despite factional squabbles, the Indian Com-

munist party was well organized; it was helped by
the rapid expansion of an unstable intelligentsia and
a rapid increase in the population, which neutralized
efforts to improve economic conditions. In later years,
communist influence increased to the degree that anti-
Western sentiment spread in the majority of the
Congress party.

Since the end of World War II, a main area in
the communist struggle for power has been the eastern-
most peninsula of southern Asia. Three to four years
of Japanese occupation had created a political vacuum
propitious for communist activities. For centuries,
Burma, Annam, and, to a lesser extent, Thailand,
Laos, and Cambodia, had gravitated within the orbit
of Chinese civilization. In Malaya, Chinese immigrants
formed the largest group of the population. Direct or
indirect European control had been disrupted by the
Japanese invasion and occupation during World War
II and traditional social structures had weakened.
These factors, together with the impetus provided by
small groups of active and dedicated communists, had
combined to make communism, in which most radical
aspirations were confluent, a primary problem.

The revolt against the French and against native
traditional authorities in Vietnam (formerly the Empire of Annam) was organized by Ho Chi Minh
(Nguyen Tat Thanh, 1890–   ), one of the ablest
Asian communists and a disciple of French communism. A common boundary with Mao's China after
the end of 1949 gave the Vietnamese communists a
considerable advantage over their opponents. In Burma
and Malaya the communists were fewer than in Vietnam. What they lacked in numbers they made up in
energy and activity. As soon as they had mustered
adequate forces, they started civil wars that lasted
several years. Less tense, in the immediate postwar

period, was the situation in Cambodia and Laos. In Thailand, Thai nationalism and a military dictatorship checked the diffusion of communism, which found followers only among the intelligentsia of the Chinese minority.

After V–J Day, communist hopes were high concerning the two large Far Eastern island nations. Guerrillas had been active in the Philippines during most of the period of Japanese occupation. Americans had been generous with supplies provided to the guerrillas, whose political tendencies were usually not known. In northern Luzon in particular, many guerrilla leaders were communists and had the loyalty of the Hukbalahaps (or Huks), whose revolutionarism was of the vague agrarian type predominant in underdeveloped countries. The establishment of an independent republic in 1946 meant that Filipino forces, not Americans, would maintain order in the islands. Intensive guerrilla warfare was waged for several years.

In Japan, communism had been repressed almost to the point of extinction during the period following the end of party rule in 1932. Just 1200 party members formed the nucleus of the postwar communist movement. Their main assets were the fellow-traveling leanings of a large section of the Socialist party (which, for a while, was divided into two independent organizations, one procommunist and the other anticommunist), the leadership they immediately established in the labor movement, and the deep hatred that sections of the population at first felt against the Americans. Guided by Nozaka, communists received 2 million votes in elections in 1946 and 3 million in 1949. Growing resistance on the part of the socialists, growing opposition in the labor unions, diminishing antagonism against Americans, and factionalism between groups headed respectively by Nozaka and Tokuda, led to a loss of influence. In the elections of October 1952, the communist vote had dropped to well below 1 million.

In the Western Hemisphere, the communist parties of the United States and Canada met with increased opposition after the end of the war. Canada did not outlaw the party, as had been done previously, but after the discovery of a spy ring of communists acting for the military intelligence of the Soviet Union, Canadian authorities kept a more careful watch on the activities of local communists. Their numbers remained small. The attempt to infiltrate Ukrainian-Canadian and Russian-Canadian communities through nationalist and religious organizations did not yield appreciable results. In some of the labor unions, communist influence remained strong, but the labor movement in general showed little tenderness for the communists. The only communist deputy in the Dominion Parliament was unseated as a result of his treasonable activities.

In the political life of the United States after the end of the war, communists remained a rather negligible, if at times vocal, element. In spite of their activity and determination, they lost most of the ground they had won in the 1930s and during the war, when, through a policy of collaboration, they had been able to gain influence in a number of organizations. The party efficiency—never great in comparison with European and some Asiatic parties—was weakened by an upheaval that had nothing to do with American problems and which occurred during the months immediately preceding and following the end of World War II. In April 1945 the French communist leader and, at the time, major spokesman for communism "J. Duclos . . . published his sensational attack upon Earl

Browder [leader of the party in the United States] . . . it was the opening move of the cold war." [9] Stalin had rightly decided that the United States was the main bulwark of democracy and should therefore, in Engel's terms, be the chief target of communist hatred and aggressiveness. These things Browder probably never understood. He was replaced by W. Z. Foster and expelled from the party in February 1946.

As a result of Soviet tactics in the United Nations, the aggressiveness of the Soviet Union and other communist-controlled countries, and an increased consciousness of the fundamental uncompatibility of the principles of democracy and communism, a wave of anticommunism swept the United States. This led to the expulsion of communists from a number of organizations and positions. The agitation was particularly strong in the labor field, where many unions "witnessed the most determined upheaval against communism." Public authorities dismissed communists and fellow-travelers from the federal and state administrations. By the end of 1947 the communists found themselves more or less isolated in the American nation. They tried a carefully staged comeback in 1948 through a new version of the "popular front," represented by the lately established Progressive party, nominally headed by the former Vice-President Henry Wallace. The Progressive party polled a little more than 1 million votes, of which only one third or less were cast by communists or convinced fellow-travelers. These numbers suffered a further decline in later years, when the evidence of Soviet aggressiveness and communist determination to acquire world control became too

[9] F. Borkenau, *European Communism,* London: Faber & Faber, Ltd., 1953, p. 456.

strong to be ignored by naive but honest former admirers. In the elections of November 1950, the last
fellow-traveler in Congress lost his seat.

The legal status of the Communist party represented one of the important problems facing the Administration, Congress, and the American nation at
the beginning of the second half of the century. Should
the party be outlawed? Could it be considered on the
same level as other political parties, functioning and
willing to go on functioning within the framework
of democratic institutions? Some legislation aimed at
curbing communist activities was passed, mainly in
1950, but the problem of the position of the communist party had been only partially solved by the
Supreme Court decision in June 1951 to recognize
the validity of the Smith Act, under which the leaders
of the American Communist party were being tried.
Between 1948 and 1952 fewer than 100 communists
were arrested; altogether about 300 were prosecuted.
Except in the case of treason trials, sentences never
exceeded five years' imprisonment.

South of the Rio Grande, communism grew unevenly. Its membership remained limited to the intelligentsia, but its influence was considerable at times.
In Mexico, the Communist party, led by D. Encinas,
was small, but for some time acted as the leader of
Latin American communism. As already noted, a
number of European refugees and exiles had strengthened it. Under the leadership of V. Toledano, an
attempt had been made to organize a Latin American
labor movement sympathetic to communism and com-
mitted to the Soviet Union. A reaction set in, however,
in the postwar period, and in January 1948 a meeting
took place in Lima, Peru, which was called by the
anticommunist labor unions of various countries, and

a new organization was established. With the elections of 1952, two decades of communist political influence in Mexico came to an end.

In Cuba, the communists controlled the labor organization to a considerable extent, but, just as in Mexico, the membership of their party was drawn overwhelmingly from the intelligentsia. Not strong enough to seize power, their policies aimed at favoring radical rightist authoritarianism against democratic groups. Since the late thirties their leader had been Blas Roca. In Guatemala the small but well-organized communist group achieved considerable political influence after the overthrow of the dictatorship of General Ubico in 1944. By 1950 Guatemala had replaced Mexico City as the main base for Latin American communism. British Guiana was another small country in which communism was strongly organized.

In Brazil, the Communist party—outlawed during the first Vargas regime—showed unexpected strength at the elections of 1946, in which it polled about 600,000 votes. Its leader, C. Prestes, became a member of the Brazilian Senate. Communism was strong in the more industrialized southern areas, where a large percentage of the population was neither of Portuguese nor mixed Portuguese-African descent, and in the populous poverty-stricken northeastern states. The bulk of the membership was drawn from the intelligentsia. In 1947 the Brazilian Government declared the aims of the Communist party to be incompatible with the constitution, and the party was outlawed. At the same time tension arose between Brazil and the Soviet Union, which led to the severing of diplomatic relations.

There was similar tension between Chile and several communist-controlled states because of the part diplomatic officials had played in fomenting strikes in the former's territory. At the 1946 presidential elections, the communists joined in a popular front with socialists and radicals. The popular front polled a majority of votes. The new president, a radical, tried to govern the country with a coalition cabinet that included the communists. The experiment lasted only a few months, after which the other parties forced the communists to withdraw from the cabinet. As in European coalition governments, the communists had used tactics detrimental to the partners in the coalition, and had made the smooth operation of democratic procedure impossible.

The communists in Bolivia were weakened by factional strife between Stalinists and Trotskyites. In Argentina, communists held an ambivalent attitude toward the dictatorship of Juan Perón. One group infiltrated the Peronista organizations and lent support to the dictatorship; another maintained an active underground organization. Elsewhere in Latin America, communism rarely reached, at that time, the proportions of a major political factor. However, in spite of setbacks in Mexico and Chile, in spite of repressive measures introduced by rightist dictatorships and the anticommunism of large sections of organized labor, communism in Latin America was stronger and better organized in 1952 than it had been in 1945. Nowhere (except, perhaps, in British Guiana) did it have a mass following, but in many countries it appealed to the emotional and unstable sections of the intelligentsia.

Officially, there were approximately 24 million members in communist parties at the beginning of 1953, 6 million of them outside the communist empire. In countries where free elections took place, the total voting strength of the communists was a little over 20 million, of whom most were to be found in France, India, Italy, and Japan. After a quarter of a century of Stalinism, communism had truly become a world-wide movement.

C H A P T E R . . . 3

The Latest Period: From Monocentrism to Polycentrism

Elements of Strength amid Vacillations

In discussing communist action, the attention of experts and the concern of statesmen is usually centered on the leadership—the personalities and official policies of communist-controlled states and communist parties. On the level of ideas, discussion revolves around Marxism-Leninism and its orthodox or heretical interpretations. In view of the authoritarian hierarchical organization of communism and the role played by ideology, the emphasis on leadership and Marxism-Leninism is justified, but if one is to acquire a correct understanding of communism today, this emphasis should not exclude other considerations.

To emphasize leadership alone tends to obscure what communism owes to the communist movement, that vast stream of millions of dedicated, hard-working, anonymous party members who carry on with their jobs no matter what happens at the top level of political responsibility. In communist-controlled countries they manage hundreds of thousands of business enterprises, or keep an alert eye on the managers of such enterprises and see to it that they do not slacken their efforts. They control hundreds of thousands of educational, cultural, labor, youth, and recreational groups. They watch their neighbors and are quick to report all signs of dissatisfaction to the police. They maintain the party machine—the central element of communist societies and of communist-controlled states—at a high level of efficiency. Outside communist-controlled countries they are the hard-working organizers, the devout missionaries of the communist cause, the able and patient infiltrators. Not all of them have read the whole of Lenin's works but they know, and have unreservedly accepted his principle, that a communist must devote himself entirely to the "cause."

Not all communists "have the passionate zeal of the Jesuit missionary, who sets out to conquer a new world for his faith," [1] but many do. Quarrels in the presidiums, secretariats, or central committees may affect party members not at all, or only indirectly and after a relatively long period. One may legitimately assume that in communist-controlled countries, in spite of careful, painstaking screening and rigid supervision, careerists and opportunists—as they are called in communist parlance—do enter the various parties; but it is unlikely that there are many. There are even fewer in the parties outside communist-controlled areas, where the communist's life is often difficult and where total devotion is essential. Sincerity of conviction is

[1] H. Laski, *Communism*, London: Butterworth & Co. (Publishers) Ltd., 1927, p. 239.

a prerequisite for admission to a communist party, acceptance in which implies a commitment as great as that demanded when joining a Christian monastic order. If party members do not receive fresh instructions because of rivalries at the top level, they carry on with their jobs on the basis of previous directives. They know what communism expects from them: disciplined action that aims at the establishment of collectivism through the seizure of political power.

For the mass of party members, Marxism-Leninism represents a few slogans, which are to communism what dogmas are to religions. The slogans help to steer the course of action. But what moves party members more than slogans is the simple vision that inspired the early Utopian socialists: the attainment of material abundance, which will eliminate suffering, conflicts, and tensions—and thereby eliminate evil as well. They know that "capitalism in its imperialistic stage"—as liberal and social democracies are described—is the main enemy, with which no compromise is possible, even if circumstances temporarily dictate the need for coexistence.

The personal commitment of millions of communists—a simple, rather mystical vision of things to come and a firm determination to realize it—must be taken into account together with leadership and Marxism-Leninism when describing communist action. An analysis of the communist movement in its early phase, possibly until Stalin's death, deals primarily with a few individuals and the situations in which they operated. Since then there has been change; with the passage of time "the movement"—the mass of anonymous communists, each doing his job whatever his station in life, or the country he lives in, whatever the effectiveness of the leaders—has become increasingly important. To this mass, communism today owes its capacity to make progress in spite of vacillations and occasional eruptions of violent factional strife among the leaders. To this mass communism owes its stability and, even more, its continuity. In 1953 the mass that made up the movement included about 24 million party members spread through all countries of all continents. Providing useful material for political maneuvering were millions of sympathizers, or fellow-travelers. Never in the history of mankind had there been such a vast group of closely integrated individuals, all bent on achieving the same goal.

In 1953 the communist movement had one outstanding feature that should be kept in mind, and another feature, which would increase in importance as years went by, had also made its appearance. The outstanding feature was the high level of cohesiveness and discipline in the communist parties—at least in relation to outside forces. Discipline is inherent in the communist idea and it enables each organized section of the movement to act as a huge well-ordered army. Cohesiveness depended on two major factors: the enthusiastic devotion of the overwhelming majority of party members, and the solidity of an efficient institutional frame. The other feature, which had already made its appearance with Tito's national-communism in Yugoslavia, was the development of autonomous centers of power within the movement. This resulted from the success achieved by communism in several areas, with relatively little direct Soviet help, in the years immediately following World War II. Sections of the communist movement with their own armed forces enjoyed autonomy—potentially if not actually. Tito's rebellion had been made possible by the elementary fact that he had an army at his command. Since 1949 there was a large communist Chinese state with its own well-equipped and well-trained armed forces. In 1953, few saw the importance of these autonomous centers of power. Tito's rebellion had had less of an impact than many in Western countries had hoped. It is true that the Yugoslav regime enjoyed a wide measure of support in its defiance of the USSR. However, the support came primarily from Yugoslav nationalists who had resented Tito as an orthodox Stalinist but approved of him as a deviationist. Few communists outside Yugoslavia had followed Tito. There had, nevertheless, been an indication of what might happen when a communist had an army at his disposal.

The movement was the core of communist strength. The states taken over by the communists formed a wide operational base for further expansion. Statistically, in 1953 communist-controlled states not only covered one fourth of the land area of the world (about two thirds of the Eurasian land mass) and embraced one third of mankind but also contributed over one sixth to the world output of goods and services, and had available one half of the world's armed forces.

Several developments in the Soviet Union are worth noting. In the first place, the crisis of World War II increased national cohesion: a Soviet nation was gradually displacing the prewar multinational state. Problems of national minorities remained and were at times troublesome (as shown by some rioting in Georgia in 1953), but they were being solved through a combination of coercion and persuasion. In the second place, uniform indoctrination, made possible by total monopoly of education and all media of communication, was reducing differences in values, ideas, and aspirations. This strengthened the effective unity that is the main goal of all who stress absolute priority of the group over the individual. Thirdly, economic losses suffered during the war had been made good by the annexation of vast and valuable European and Asiatic territories. A process of economic growth, particularly in heavy industry—the key to military power—was taking place. The Soviet Union could be considered stronger in every aspect in 1953 than when it had been attacked by Germany in 1941.

The process of political consolidation, prerequisite to economic growth, was well advanced in the eight European People's Democracies and Democratic Republics (indistinguishable from the dictatorships of the proletariat). In three states particularly (Poland, East Germany, Hungary) there were elements of unrest within groups the communists could not hope to assimilate and which had not been totally eliminated because of their sheer size. However, the communist organization supported by Soviet troops was strong enough to cope with them. In the Far East, communist power was strongly entrenched in the Mongolian, North Korean, and Chinese People's Republics.

China was in the midst of ruthless repression and suppression. There had been the suppression of economic classes (landowners, independent farmers above the level of total destitution, former owners of industrial and commercial enterprises). There was the continuing repression of national minorities (numbering 35–40 million people on the Chinese mainland), and unrelenting economic and social pressure against both the traditional (largely Confucian) and the Westernized sectors of the intelligentsia. Chinese communists were determined to gain quickly the control that Soviet communism had taken twenty years to achieve (from the organization of the Cheka under Lenin to the purges under Stalin). In 1953 they seemed to be well along the road to success. The intervention in

Korea had strengthened unity within China. In Chinese eyes it looked like an outstanding military and diplomatic success against "imperialism" and "capitalism," and had increased the prestige of the new revolutionary leadership. Chinese prestige and influence were also growing rapidly among revolutionary groups in all underdeveloped countries: here was concrete evidence that even an economically backward, nonwhite nation could successfully industralize and defy even the strongest Western capitalistic power—the United States. More important for future developments in the late fifties and in the sixties was the fact that Soviet vacillations in 1950 and Chinese determination had strengthened the position of Chinese vis-à-vis Soviet communism. Peiping was rapidly rivalling Moscow as a center directing revolutionary activities in large areas of the world. Asian and African communists, or would-be communists, and many Latin Americans, felt more at home with the Chinese than with the Russians. Noncommunist progressives often felt the fascination of the new-found Chinese dynamism.

Outside the communist bloc, developments at the ideological level (important for revolutionaries) that would favor a further expansion of communism were taking place. In the advanced democratic nations, success in the economic field (a widespread high standard of living and rapid economic expansion in most of continental Europe) was accompanied by growing intellectual apathy. By and large, the intelligentsia of Western nations was unwilling to commit itself to the ideology which, founded on the principle of individual liberty, had spurred the revolutionary transformation and the progress of the West in modern times. This is not to say that most of the Western intelligentsia had abandoned the ideology. But doubts, a dose of skepticism, and excessive stress on fault-

finding, made it difficult for Westerners to compete
with communist intellectual dynamism. How could
one convince others if unsure of one's own convictions? (American leaders have emphasized again and
again that besides economic and military competition
between Western and communist nations, there is
ideological competition—and that this may be even
more important). Strong economically and militarily,
the West was growing ideologically weaker—on both
sides of the Atlantic.

This weakness was particularly crucial in relation
to the nations in the underdeveloped areas of the
world. Here, more and more people were thinking, facing their problems, looking for solutions. Arabs, Indians, and a few others could find in their own cultural
backgrounds elements to be used to formulate ideas
and find solutions. For hundreds of millions endowed
with poorer cultural traditions, political and economic
ideas had to come from the outside. The age-old
division between East and West had become in practical terms a choice between communism and democracy. Communists were articulate, convinced, and therefore convincing; democrats from Western nations were
inarticulate, unconvinced, and unconvincing. It is not
surprising that the impact of communist ideology stood
a good chance of being considerably more effective than
that of the West. In the underdeveloped world the
ferment caused by rising expectations and deep
emotionalism was on the increase. It expressed itself
increasingly through radical extremism and violent
revolutionism—both in the vast colonial areas still
held by Europeans and in the underdeveloped states
of Latin America, the Middle East, southern Asia.
The aspirations of the modern progressive West,
centered on the autonomy of the individual and the
individual's right to self-realization in all fields of

endeavor, failed to channel the ferment. Instead, the ferment was channeled by aspirations and values that made communism more acceptable than democracy to many.

Communists were aware in the early fifties that a new opportunity for them was in the making. Just as the disintegration of the Russian empire had created a political vacuum that the Bolsheviki had filled in 1917–1921 and the disintegration of the German and Japanese empires had created in Eastern Europe and the Far East more political vacuums that communists had again filled in 1944–1949, so the disintegration of European colonial empires was creating new areas of political vacuum, vaster than the combined area of the Soviet Union and China. The situation looked favorable and the opportunity was not to be missed.

The Year Stalin Died (1953)

Shortly before his death, on the occasion of the 19th congress of the CPSU (the first since 1939), Stalin wrote on *Economic Problems of Socialism in the USSR*. This essay provided communists with a meaningful synthesis of Stalinist ideas and policies. Certainly he "was a . . . wiser Stalin than the one who . . . had . . . told on April 13, 1928 that there is no fortress in the world which . . . the Bolsheviks cannot take." [2] Whatever may have been the personal fears and obsessions of a man fast growing old, Stalin's mind was lucid, and the pamphlet published at the end of 1952 helped his successors to steer their way in a

[2] J. S. Reshetar, *A Concise History of the Communist Party of the Soviet Union*, New York: Frederick A. Praeger, Inc., 1960, p. 252.

world that was being rapidly transformed by political, technological, and ideological changes.

In restating the final goals of communism and emphasizing the need to eliminate everything non-communist sooner or later, Stalin was a loyal Leninist. But where tactics were concerned he departed from Lenin's teachings when he declared, in the involved communist jargon, that a major war was unlikely (because of the deterrent effect of nuclear weapons). Reinterpreting Engels, relentless pressure, short of war, should be exercised against the United States. At the same time peace must be stressed, blandishments of all kinds should be used to create a gulf between democratic and underdeveloped states and to cause tension within the democratic camp. The unity of the communist bloc should be strengthened.

Dangerous brinkmanship was being practiced in foreign affairs. In the internal affairs of communist states and of the communist movement, ruthless repression was the norm everywhere during the months following the 19th congress of the CPSU. This was evidenced by trials against supposed deviationists in Czechoslovakia, a wave of arrests in East Germany, the denunciation of the doctors' plot in Moscow, class liquidation in China, expulsion- of old-time party members from the French Communist party, among other developments.

On March 5, 1953, Stalin died. There was considerable speculation about the manner of his death, and the truth will probably never be known. Communists were stunned: for too long, a quarter of a century, communism and Stalinism had been one. The masses of communists and fellow-travelers everywhere grieved; however strange it may seem, the rank and file loved him. A sigh of relief, instead, went up among large sectors of the Soviet communist oligarchy. Being closer to the center of power, many had been alarmed by what had seemed, in 1952, a prelude to new large-scale purges. Loyalty to Stalin was no guarantee against arrest and execution. Noncommunists everywhere hoped for a change.

The immediate problem in Moscow was the reorganization of the government. There had been times when an heir apparent had seemed to be in the making: Kirov in the early 1930s, Zhdanov (1896–1948) in the middle 1940s. But there was no heir apparent in 1953. Power was unevenly distributed among a few of Stalin's closest collaborators: Beria (1899–1953), the head of the police, Malenkov (1902–   ), the head of the party machinery, Molotov, an old Bolshevik and Stalin's chief trouble shooter in international affairs, Kaganovich, Stalin's brother-in-law and a chief expert in industrial planning, Mikoyan, the able head of an important sector of the economy, Bulganin (1895–   ), a political general, Voroshilov (1881–   ), a respected military and political figure, and a few others. Not many people abroad were acquainted with the name of N. S. Khrushchev (1894–   ), who had been very close to Stalin since January 1938, a Russian who had headed the party organization in the Ukraine at the time when the overwhelming majority of the members of the Central Committee of the Ukrainian Communist party had been executed. A few World War II military leaders enjoyed considerable prestige in the armed forces, Marshal Zhukov (1896–   ) most of all. With Stalin's death, the exercise of power devolved automatically on the members of the Presidium (the former Political Bureau) of the CPSU. Thus began the period of "collective leadership" characterized by intense strife among the few men who composed it.

Again, as in 1924–1927, no one can say how much the factional struggle at the top (the only place in a communist state where factional struggle can take place) was due to personal ambitions and fears and how much to dissension on questions of internal and external policy. "There were at least four major issues upon which divergences of views between members of the Presidium were evident . . . the perennial question of the relative importance to be attached to the production of means of production and to the production of consumer goods . . . agricultural policy . . . decentralization of control over industry [instead] of improved centralized control . . . relations with Yugoslavia." To these issues must, of course, be added issues of foreign policy, chiefly the pros and cons of the "prospect of achieving peacefully the universal victory of communism." [3] We know that some of the people involved in the factional struggle, for instance, Molotov and Kaganovich, held steadfastly to at least some of their positions; that others switched with the greatest of ease from one position to another, Khrushchev more easily than anyone else. Whatever the reasons, dissensions soon appeared in the Soviet "collective leadership." At the end of June all the weaker members of the collective leadership were already ganged together against the strongest, Beria. The former all-powerful head of the police—an empire within an empire—was arrested, and executed in December, together with many of his supporters.

A good deal has been written about a "thaw" in the Soviet Union following Stalin's death. There was, indeed, some relaxation of the pressure exercised by the state and the party in relation to national minorities, to intellectual activities, and to supposedly dissident communists. (Later, the word revisionism was

[3] L. Schapiro, *The Communist Party of the Soviet Union*, New York: Random House, Inc., 1960, pp. 553-559.

used to describe—and condemn—this relaxation). As there was a "thaw" in the Soviet Union, so there was in the countries it directly controlled, that is, the European satellites. Justifiable wishful thinking in Western countries and among the anticommunist majorities in the satellites sometimes interpreted the "thaw" as evidence of a change of heart in Soviet communism, the result of an internal process of liberalization. A similar illusion had already made its appearance several times before, most recently during World War II. In point of fact, there had been no liberalization, any more than there had been in 1921–1925 or 1941–1944.

In 1953–1956 the factional struggle for succession weakened the efficiency of the leadership. The inefficiency in turn caused a loosening (though not much) in the coercive power of the state. The "thaw" was not anything the communists wanted; it simply happened because those whose function it was to make decisions were quarrelling. An unexpected result of the partial paralysis in the communist leadership was the revolt of June 17, 1953 in East Berlin, which soon spread to many localities of East Germany. The revolt was a serious one and casualties were numerous. But Soviet troops stationed in East Germany, supported by East German military units, had little difficulty in defeating the rebels, who had counted on aid from the West (that is, the United States). The West was not in a position to give this aid, for psychological more than for military or political reasons.

The foreign policy of the members of the communist bloc followed, in the main, the lines traced by Stalin at the end of 1952. There was the unrelenting pressure on Western powers, of which the most concrete expression was the downing of American and British planes. No less concrete, but more subtle, was the aid

Soviet and Chinese communists supplied to nationalist movements in colonial and former colonial areas, the support given extreme in contrast to more moderate nationalists, and the adoption of a large-scale program for the training of Africans in particular. What had been done for Far Eastern revolutionism in the early twenties was going to be done for African revolutionism, with training institutes in Moscow, Peiping, Prague. There was stress on peace. All kinds of congresses, whose main theme was peace, met in communist capitals: labor, youth, women's, student, and cultural congresses. The Korean armistice, signed July 27, 1953, was presented by the communists as clear evidence that peace was their main preoccupation. Many non-communists believed it. The Soviet leadership also decided to do what Stalin could not have done: to re-establish friendly relations with Tito of Yugoslavia and to attempt the reabsorption of Titoism, or national-communism, in the Soviet-led world communist movement. Molotov alone opposed this policy and continued to consider Titoist revisionism incompatible with Marxism-Leninism.

By the time Stalin died it had become evident that communist hopes of further improvement in the position of their movement in Western democratic nations were not going to materialize. The hopes had been high during World War II and the immediate postwar period. The democratic West included at the time the European and Mediterranean democracies, the English-speaking nations of North America and Australasia, and Latin American states in which democratic institutions had taken root. In spite of the fact that communism was still an important factor in the political life of half a dozen countries, the democratic West seemed to become more and more impervious to it.

The role of the French Communist party in the communist movement had been considerable for a long time. From Syria to Morocco, Arab communists had learned their communism from France more than from the Soviet Union. This was true also of many African and Asian communists (among the latter, mention should be made of Teng Hsiao-ping, 1902–   , later Secretary-general of the Chinese Communist party and, in 1963, head of the Chinese delegation that debated in Moscow with Soviet communists). But in 1947–1953 the membership of the French Communist party dropped by about half, from close to a million to a little over half a million. In spite of the considerable electoral strength of the party, its influence on French politics was relatively small. This strange, and important, phenomenon has been interpreted in different ways. One element leading to near-apathy was probably the contradiction troubling the minds of sincere French Marxist-Leninists: more communists among the intelligentsia in France than anywhere else were realizing the incompatibility between the vision that inspired them and the reality of communist-controlled states. Not until some time after the 1958 triumph of De Gaulle did French communists begin to shake off their apathy.

In elections in Germany in 1953 the communist vote declined from the 5.7 percent of 1949 to 2.2 percent. There was a similar decline in Austria. An exception to the general rule of communist weakening in Western democracies seemed to be Italy, where problems unconnected with communism enabled the Communist party to strengthen its position at the general elections of 1953. In the English-speaking nations of the Commonwealth, communists were reduced to a few tens of thousands.

In the United States, first Senator McCarthy and

then the Republican party achieved success in riding the crest of a huge anticommunist wave. Whatever may have been the rights and wrongs of McCarthyism, that was the period when a considerable number of American party members and fellow-travelers did what they should have done sooner: they thought seriously about communism. Most of them discovered (and were bewildered by the discovery) that they had been the victims of a mirage, that neither Marxism-Leninism on the theoretical level, nor the Soviet Union, the satellites, Red China, or Yugoslavia on the practical level, corresponded to what they had ingenuously thought communism to be. Anticommunist slogans of the 1952 presidential campaign were taken literally by many people outside the United States. Lack of American aid to those who rose against communist domination in Eastern Europe, in 1953 and afterwards, caused disillusionment and bitter resentment.

In Latin America an anticommunist uprising was put down by the fellow-traveling government of President Arbenz in Guatemala in 1953. Elections were held in British Guiana in view of forthcoming independence, and the winner was the party led by the communists or near-communists Jagan (1918–   ) and his American-born wife. British government intervention then put an end to the brief period of rule by Jagan's party (which was, however, resumed in 1961). In Perón's Argentina, Vargas's Brazil, and Batista's Cuba, well-organized, clandestine communist parties acted on the old principle, applied until 1934 in Europe, that radical rightist dictatorships are preferable to democracy. Perón's party was, and has since remained —either as a legal or an illegal organization—infiltrated with communists and fellow-travelers. In Brazil the communists infiltrated Vargas's Labor party. In Cuba relations between the Communist party and

Batista's military dictatorship deteriorated after the
Soviet Union broke off diplomatic relations in 1952.
The communist Partido Socialista Popular was outlawed, but the illegal communist organization survived and many "Cuban Communists actually entered
Batista's own party. Batista and his associates were
happy to have these new recruits." [4] Growing activity,
then apparently directed from Guatemala, compensated for small numbers (a few hundred or at most
a few thousand in each case) in several other Latin
American countries—particularly Bolivia and Venezuela.

In the colonial, ex-colonial and independent underdeveloped countries of Africa, Asia, and the Middle
East (covering about one third of the world's land
area), communism, undisturbed by what was happening
in Moscow, was in general in ascendancy and made
gains in 1953:

There were some setbacks, especially in the Philippines
and Malaya. In the Philippines, American-trained and
American-equipped Filipino troops considerably reduced the
area in which the Huks had been operating since World
War II. Of the Huks, only the leaders were convinced communists. The surrender of Taruc in 1954 ended the revolt,
except for a few pockets here and there. In British Malaya,
communist guerrillas, led by Chen Ping and presumably
supplied by Chinese communists, had been active since 1948.

By the end of 1953, military operations, efficiently organized
by British jungle fighters, had destroyed most of the nearly
inaccessible bases from which the communists operated. On
the increase, instead, were the activities of communists south
of Malaya, in Singapore, where the population is mostly
Chinese.

[4] R. J. Alexander, *Communism in Latin America*, New Brunswick, N.J.: Rutgers University Press, 1957, p. 293.

The armistice signed in Panmunjom, which ended hostilities in Korea, had considerable impact beyond the Korean peninsula. It gave respite at last to the American-protected Republic of Korea. It also consolidated communist hold in North Korea (whence more than 1 million people had fled south.) More important, the armistice enabled Chinese communists to bolster their defenses in the Strait of Formosa and to increase their aid to the communists in Vietnam. (The victory of Ho Chi Minh in North Vietnam in 1954 and the Formosa crisis of April 1955 were both related to the 1953 Korean armistice).

In Indonesia, where nationalists had fought communists in 1949, the agreement negotiated by the able communist leader Aidit created a united communist-nationalist front against the democratic socialists and the two large Islamic parties that had support among the population. The communists started as the junior members of the united front: they worked hard to become senior members.

In Burma, the White Flag or orthodox communists led by Than Tun tried to reach an agreement with some of the ethnic minorities, the Kachin and the Karen. Despite a good deal of factional strife, the Indian Communist party led by Ghosh continued to make significant progress, especially in the southern states of the Union. Outlawing communist activities scarcely affected them in Pakistan, Nepal, and Iran.

Among Arab countries, Syria continued to have the most efficient communist organization. French communists had trained communist organizers in the still dependent countries of the Maghreb, and their activities were on the increase. The communist underground was gaining adherents in Iraq, particularly among the educated people of the Kurdish minority.

Little was known in the West about communism in Africa south of the Sahara, but among the few educated Africans

Marxism-Leninism had considerable impact, both as a theory explaining their position and justifying their hatreds, and as a program giving direction to revolutionary efforts. Africans had been to the Soviet Union and others were now going to China. They were indoctrinated ideologically, and trained practically, for revolutionary activities. In 1953, they were not many, but through them communism was making its appearance in Negro Africa. The year Stalin died communists were looking to the future confidently.

The Second Struggle for Succession: toward Polycentrism (1954-1957)

For a while after the arrest of Beria (accused of being a traitor since 1919!) and his chief supporters, little was heard about events at the first and second levels of the Soviet leadership: the Presidium, the Party Secretariat, the Central Committee of the CPSU. Many thought that a new, benevolent era had come to stay. The year 1954 was Malenkov's; he advocated a "new look" centered on two themes: a better life for the Soviet people (and the people in the satellite states), and peaceful coexistence with "capitalism." Consumers were told there would be more goods available, farmers that they would no longer be discriminated against and that in *agrorod* (agrarian cities) they would be as well-off as industrial workers. The celebration of the 300th anniversary of the union of the Ukraine with Russia became an occasion for praises of Soviet national minorities. Scientists criticized Stalin's protégé Lysenko, and musicians criticized Khatchaturian. The year 1954 saw the publication of books hurriedly written by Ehrenburg, Panova, and other staunch communist writers criticizing—indirectly —terrorism, the poverty of the masses, the careerism of party members. The "thaw" seemed well set in. But by December, authors were already being warned not to stray too far. In January 1955 Shepilov (1905–   ), spokesman for a majority of Presidium members, wrote an article in which he criticized Malenkov's economic policies. At a meeting of party leaders, Khrushchev, the new star, attacked Malenkov in the name of heavy industry and on the ground that stress on consumer goods was a betrayal of communism. (In simpler terms, the faction for which Khrushchev spoke wanted greater military preparedness.) Malenkov was demoted (but, unlike Beria, remained alive as he was considerably less dangerous). Like Stalin thirty years earlier, Khrushchev had devoted his energies to the party organization and had put his own followers in key positions.

The next two and a half years were the years of B and K: Bulganin was Prime Minister and Khrushchev the First Secretary of the party. In the reduced collective leadership, Molotov represented a slightly dissident element. He was for heavy industry (that is, a high level of war preparedness) and therefore opposed to Malenkov. He was also for greater direct aggressiveness against "capitalist" countries, in disagreement with Khrushchev, who had made Malenkov's foreign policy wholeheartedly his own. Compelled to recant publicly in October of 1955, Molotov lost prestige. Khrushchev was supposed to have the support of three of the most influential army leaders, Zhukov, Konev (1897–   ), Vasilevksy (1895–   ). Internally, capital investment was switched from agriculture and consumer goods to heavy industry, scientific research, and space exploration. Externally, the Soviet satellite bloc was strengthened in 1955 by the Eastern Security Treaty, or Warsaw Pact, which established a better integrated military organization (the answer to West Germany's membership in NATO). At the same time a policy of peaceful coexistence was pursued, with the peace treaty that gave Austria back her independence, the transfer of the base of Porkkala to Finland, and the establishment of diplomatic relations with the German Federal Republic (West Germany). Khrushchev and Bulganin went to Belgrade in May and to India later in the year. They approved of, and promoted, "cultural" exchanges with capitalistic and underdeveloped countries (participation in scientific congresses, tournées of artists, visas for tourists). A policy of economic aid to foreign countries, both communist and noncommunist (loans to Yugoslavia and North Vietnam, machinery to Afghanistan and India, and so forth) began to be applied on a large scale in 1955. The climax of the year was the Geneva Summit Conference of July and the ensuing (short-lived) "spirit of Geneva."

At the beginning of 1956 came a bombshell. The 20th party congress, attended by representatives of all communist parties in the world, was held in Moscow in February. Khrushchev delivered the opening speech, an indication that he was first among his peers of the collective leadership. On the 18th, Mikoyan expressed in his speech some criticism of Stalinist policies. On the 25th, at a final closed session, Khrushchev made a long impassioned speech exposing Stalin as a cruel dictator and a man who had harmed the communist cause. What was exposed was neither new nor startling nor complete for noncommunists. But repercussions were considerable among communists who came to know of the speech. A copy of this had found its way outside communist countries, and a few months later the content became available to the public.

Communists had always denied reports of terrorism, massacres, arbitrariness, and other features of Soviet despotism: "the official admission that they were substantially true undermined for a time their faith in their leadership." [5] Fellow-travelers everywhere had accepted communist denials at their face value. Khrushchev made no mention in his speech of terrorism applied to noncommunists. They were unimportant chattels. But he spoke of the liquidation of loyal Marxist-Leninists—and even good communists could consider this a crime. Worse, there had been executions of Stalinists—and all the 1956 Soviet leaders had been Stalinists. Khrushchev's speech of February 25th is memorable because it broke, at least for the time being and possibly forever, the unity of the communist movement. Tito, national-communists generally, and a few other dissidents applauded. But in all communist parties there were groups that resented the attack on Stalin, and among those who resented it most strongly were the leaders in two autonomous centers of communist power: huge China and little Albania.

Why the speech? It is doubtful that there was on Khrushchev's part "a deliberate attempt to attribute . . . excesses and bloodshed to . . . one man . . . in order to remove responsibility for these crimes from the Party." [6] The communist mentality is not concerned with that type of crime. The most probable explanation is represented by the succession of events: Khrushchev had joined the group that had ganged up against Beria; he had led the group that ousted Malenkov and opposed Molotov; now the remaining members of the "collective leadership" were ganging up against him.

It is known that in any hierarchical authoritarian structure, the lower level of authority automatically

---

[5] L. Schapiro, *op. cit.*, p. 560.
[6] J. S. Reshetar, Jr., *op. cit.*, p. 271.

assumes power that the higher level is unwilling or unfit to exercise. In the specific case, the highest level was the Presidium and the Party Secretariat, and there factionalism had caused paralysis; the level below, represented by the Central Committee, was not functioning; power to take decisions was vested, exceptionally, in the Party Congress. The mood of the Congress was for the end of terrorism (but only the terrorism directed at orthodox communists, that is, ex-Stalinists!). Mikoyan's guarded remarks of February 18th, expressing mild criticisms of Stalin, had been received enthusiastically. A majority in the Congress might have turned against Khrushchev, who had been Stalin's close collaborator for fifteen years. Khrushchev and his clique of supporters could save themselves only by taking the lead in attacking Stalin's excesses. A personal quarrel among ambitious and ruthless men was having political repercussions.

With his speech Khrushchev and his friends did save themselves. However, it took Khrushchev another year and a half to consolidate his position. As is customary among communists, he identified himself with a program, a simple one: maximum emphasis on the rapid growth of heavy industry on the home front, a high level of military preparedness, the end of the "thaw" in the USSR and its satellites; in external relations, continuation of the peaceful coexistence recommended by Stalin and practiced by Malenkov. Early in 1957 he obtained the approval of the Presidium for a radical reorganization of the economy. This helped in the remarkable achievements of heavy industry during the next few years, in strengthening the Soviet Union militarily, and in making a success of space exploration. But his opponents were banding together: "In June 1957, Khrushchev, having been outvoted in the Presidium and threatened with removal from the Secretariat, succeeded in summoning an extraordinary meeting of the full Central Committee in which he could rely on adequate support." [7] A majority in the Central Committee supported Khrushchev in his attack against a so-called antiparty group. To Malenkov and Molotov, who had tried comebacks, were added Kaganovich and Shepilov. They were not executed, but expelled from the leadership now controlled by Khrushchev. Bulganin quietly faded into the background. In October Marshal Zhukov was demoted while visiting Albania. The crisis caused by Stalin's death was over, for the time being. Successful against his opponents, master of the Soviet industrial machinery, basking in the reflected glory of Sputnik (October 4, 1957), Khrushchev and his clique had triumphed—but at a price. They had broken the unity of the communist movement. Powerful in the Soviet Union and its satellites, Khrushchev will never enjoy the position of leader of world communism that Lenin and Stalin held.

Until 1956–1957 the communist leadership of the European satellites, of the minor Asian states controlled by communists, and of China was subordinate to that of the Soviet Union. World communism had been directed since 1943 by the Presidium of the CPSU with the collaboration of a few prominent communists from other countries. During 1956–1957, factionalism in Moscow led first to a series of disturbances and then to a weakening in the cohesion of the communist bloc. Because of the rigid control exercised by a unified and loyal local leadership, the impact of Soviet events was felt little at the time in Bulgaria, Czechoslovakia, East Germany, Mongolia, North Korea, North Vietnam, and Rumania. In the rest of the com-

[7] L. Schapiro, *op. cit.*, p. 561.

munist bloc, however, there were soon serious developments.

In Poland and Hungary communists were still faced, in 1956, with considerable difficulties. They lacked the mass following that existed in Czechoslovakia and eastern Asia. It is true that since the repressions of the late forties there had been no organized political opposition in the two countries. But there was resistance, on the part of intellectuals opposed to censorship, on the part of Catholics opposed to atheism, of peasants opposed to collectivization. In Warsaw and Budapest the communist leadership was divided into "hards" and "softs": the former advocated harsh measures reminiscent of Lenin's terrorism and war communism; the latter favored policies closer to those of Lenin's first few months in power and of the NEP. Several Titoist sympathizers had been executed, but an underground Titoist current survived. These, among others, were the factors that provided a foundation for factionalism, and the weakening of Soviet control—due to interparty strife in Moscow—facilitated its increase. The result was semiparalysis in the parties of the two countries in 1956. Semiparalysis meant governmental inefficiency. This, in turn, meant that noncommunists and anticommunists had greater possibilities for action.

There were strikes in Poland in June and considerable open agitation in Hungary in October. In Poland, however, the timely death of the Stalinist Bierut (1892–1956) allowed the Polish communist leadership to rally round Bierut's opponent Gomulka (1905–   ). Because of the communists' partial loss of control, concessions had to be made to the peasantry, the Catholic Church, the intellectuals. Thanks to this tactical withdrawal of the communists, Poland escaped a revolution, though it had come pretty close. In Hungary the rift between two opposing factions, one led by the Stalinist

Rakosi and the other by Nagy (1896–1958), was more
serious than in Poland and lasted longer. The agitation
of noncommunists became a revolution late in October.
For about ten days the Hungarians were free once
again. The new regime, a coalition led by Nagy, asked
for help. No help came from the United Nations, the
United States, or Yugoslavia. Early in November,
Soviet troops intervened and re-established communist
control. Soviet intervention in Hungary caused a minor
crisis among communists in democratic countries and
a major one among fellow-travelers. A major crisis
of a different kind occurred among noncommunists
in satellite countries, whose hopes of freeing themselves
were shattered and who lost confidence in Western
democracies.

In China there had always been more of a collective
leadership than in the Soviet Union. Since the middle
1930s, cohesion in the leadership had been remarkable.
Chou En-lai (1898–   ), Chu-Teh, Liu Shao-chi
(1898–   ), Chen-Yi (1902–   ), Teng Hsiao-ping,
and others shared power with Mao. In Peiping the
factional quarrel among Soviet leaders was looked
upon with serious misgivings. Chinese delegates had
listened carefully to Khrushchev's speech; they hoped,
apparently, that unity would be re-established in Moscow. As unity was not forthcoming and—in view of
problems to be solved—the need to clarify positions
was becoming more and more pressing, the Chinese
leadership, after having tried for nearly a year to
maintain a deferential attitude towards Moscow, came
out on the side of the Stalinists.

This decision of the Chinese communists is not
surprising, inasmuch as their internal and external
policies were replicas of those of Stalin in the early
thirties: the forced total collectivization of agriculture,
a forced pace of development in mining and heavy
industry, a maximum of military preparedness, the

ruthless liquidation of all nonassimilated or non-assimilable groups, an intransigence toward "capitalist" countries (with greater aggressiveness exemplified after Stalin's death by intervention in Indochina in 1953–1954 and in the 1955 Formosa Strait crisis), accompanied by subversive infiltration in the underdeveloped sections of the world. However temporary, partial, and expedient, Malenkov's and Khrushchev's policy of pseudocoexistence with "capitalism" had no supporters in Peiping. A statement praising Stalin came out in December 1956. With the declaration of the 8th party congress on Marxism-Leninism as a guide to action and not a dogma, and with Mao's speech of February 27, 1957, the Chinese leaders left the door open to unity of the communist bloc; but the more Khrushchev's faction strengthened its hold in the Soviet Union, the more autonomous Chinese communism became. At the western end of the communist world, a process similar to that in China developed in small and isolated Albania.

The new situation was described by the Italian communist leader Togliatti, a man influential among non-Italian communists, as *polycentrism*. By the end of 1957 there were three separate and independent major centers of communist power: Moscow, Peiping, Belgrade. A fourth, in Poland, had been hoped for by non-communists but failed to materialize—some say because Polish communists did not possess the means, that is, the armed forces, to assert their independence. It more likely was because the faction that triumphed in Poland agreed with most other European communists that everything should be sacrificed to unity. Whatever the motivations and the rationalizations, four and a half years after Stalin's death the communist ice shelf had broken into several icebergs. The material (ideology and institutions) composing all the icebergs was essentially the same, but icebergs floating separately create one kind of situation, and a solid ice shelf creates a quite different one. In each communist-controlled state factionalism had been curbed; but factionalism had disrupted the communist bloc. However, no one was in a position, either in 1957 or in the years immediately after, to evaluate the importance of the disruption in relation to the over-all communist movement.

In 1954–1957 communism continued to lose ground in Western democracies. Except in Finland, Greece, and (to a lesser extent) Iceland, the loss was both in numbers and in dynamism. It was due only in very small measure to the post-Stalin factional struggle (although this had had a considerable impact on the French Communist party, for instance). More important was the economic "miracle" of continental Europe and the realization that through welfare measures and the introduction of so-called stabilizers, economic security and stability could be achieved within the frame of democratic institutions. Most important of all was the fact already mentioned in relation to the United States: Many, particularly among the intelligentsia, had embraced communism in the thirties and forties in the sincere conviction that communism was the road to fulfillment of the aspirations and goals of the democratic West; belatedly, they realized that communism was the total negation of such goals and aspirations.

In France, the communists found a new element of cohesion and a new field of activity in the aid given to Algerian Moslem nationalists after the outbreak of the Algerian insurrection (November 1954). French communism was the nationalists' main ally in their seven and a half years' struggle. In Italy there was a decline in party membership, a weakening of communist influence in the labor movement, and—

more important—the gradual loosening of the ties which, since the war years, had bound left-wing Italian socialists to the communists; this situation lasted ten years, until early 1963, when a revival occurred. In the United States, the Communist Control Act of 1954 was the logical outcome of the growing anticommunism among all sections of the population: Americans actually tended to exaggerate the threat represented by their communists. In the English-speaking countries of the Commonwealth, communism remained, intellectually and politically, a negligible factor. Labor, youth, peace, and other organizations, set up and led by Americans, broke the monopoly that the communists had tried to establish in the respective world organizations.

In Latin America the mid-fifties represent—on the surface—a lull in communist progress. This was not the result of events in Moscow, but of the determined action of anticommunist groups. The conference of the Organization of American States, held in Caracas in March 1954, approved an anticommunist resolution expressing the member-states' determination to curb communist activities. In June of the same year the dictatorial regime of the fellow-traveling Arbenz in Guatemala was overthrown by exiles based in Nicaragua and Honduras. Since Guatemala had replaced Mexico City as the main center of communist activities in Latin America, the political change disrupted the communist organization for a while. As an important section of Argentinian communists, led by Real and Puiggros, had cooperated with Perón, the latter's downfall in 1955, coupled with the anticommunism of the military and of the majority Radical party, led to a temporary eclipse of the communists in Argentina. In Cuba, Batista jailed the communists who did not cooperate with him, and kept a careful eye on those who did. In Chile, the small Communist party, despite ample funds, was unable to make headway or to weaken the political hold of conservative forces. In Mexico, the Communist party was only a faint image of what it had been during the presidencies of Cardenas and Camacho; communists and fellow-travelers in the administration were dismissed. Only in Brazil, where communists supported Goulart, the successor of President Vargas (a suicide in August 1954), did communism seem to increase its influence. But it was only a lull, as later events were to show.

In several of the newly independent and nearly independent countries of Asia and Africa, communists —undisturbed by what was going on in Moscow or between Moscow, Belgrade, and Peiping—made considerable progress:

The 1954 Geneva agreement that ended French rule in Indochina and gave to Ho's communists and nationalists the control of North Vietnam was a decisive victory for the communists and made up for losses in the Philippines and Malaya. The French having departed, the Americans were compelled to take over the defense of South Vietnam, where about 1 million North Vietnamese (mostly Catholic converts) had fled. In 1954, not to be alone in protecting southern Asia from communism, the Americans organized SEATO, a pale and not very efficient imitation of NATO (and gave their support to another, even paler, imitation, METO— later CENTO—which aimed at checking communist pressures in western Asia).

In 1955, communist guerrillas based in North Vietnam occupied two northern provinces of Laos. This initiated an action that ended temporarily in 1962 with the so-called neutralization of the country—actually its partial handing-over to a precarious coalition in which communists were the most influential group. Membership in the Burmese Communist party increased threefold, but the faction-torn leadership was unable to take advantage of the situation. Fellow-traveling "neutralists" came into power in still another Buddhist country, Ceylon.

In the only free elections ever held in Indonesia (October 1955) the Communist party received 22 percent of the votes: the nationalists in control of the country became more and more dependent on their communist allies, the moving spirit of Indonesia's "guided democracy." In due time there was the suppression of opposition parties—of democratic socialists and of both traditionalist and progressive Moslems—and the abolition of political freedom.

In India, in 1955, the communists received 30 percent of the vote in the newly-established state of Andhra, and in 1957 they achieved a plurality in Kerala, which they governed for two years. Communist activities were on the increase in Pakistan. Syria remained the chief base for the communist organization in Arab countries, particularly in those, like Iraq, which were also located in the Fertile Crescent. Repressive measures were adopted against native communists by the Egyptian dictatorship, led since 1954 by Nasser, and by the governments of newly-independent Tunisia and Morocco. Little was heard as yet of communism in Africa south of the Sahara, except that many young Africans found their way to the Soviet Union and Czechoslovakia (and others, in unknown numbers, to China), and that communist agents seemed to be at work instigating riots and a minor civil war in Cameroon.

The New Course (1958-   ):
Internal Developments

Stalin's death had strained communist parties, but without seriously affecting their hold on countries they controlled or their capacity to expand in several areas of the world. Tensions within the high echelons of the communist leadership had reached a climax in the events of 1956 and had relaxed considerably by the end of 1957, while leaving open the way to future schisms. But it would be wrong to assume that communism had changed on either the ideological or the practical level. Internal developments in communist-controlled states described in this section show that the policies of polycentric communism were not essentially different from those of the previous era.

The years immediately following 1957 witness, in each of the major sections into which communism was now divided organizationally, an effort to return to the origins, to Leninism, in order to eliminate the debilitating effects of the political vacillations of the 1953–1957 period and of the intellectual "thaw." Ideology, goals, and basic institutions did not differ in Soviet, Maoist, and Titoist communism. There was agreement on Leninism among all communists. One can go further: "the four pillars of Stalinism were, and are: agrarian collectivism; state management of industry; one-party state control; and imperialism." [8] Concerning these four pillars there was no dissent among the leaders of communist-controlled states in the late fifties and early sixties. A Czech communist could write that "the dictatorship of the proletariat in Czechoslovakia differs from the form adopted by the October Socialist revolution . . . by the recognition of the former bourgeois parliamentary institutions." [9] The difference was superficial, and meaningless. The substance of the Czechoslovak regime after February

[8] L. Fisher, *Russia Revisited*, New York: Doubleday & Company, Inc. 1957, p. 81.

[9] J. Kozak, *And Not a Shot Was Fired*, New Canaan, Conn.; Long House, 1962, p. 45.

1948 was identical to that of the Russian regime that
followed the October 1917 revolution.

After the jolt caused by the Hungarian revolution
of October-November 1956, communists agreed that
the first thing to do was to heed Lenin once again:
"The dictatorship of the proletariat is . . . the most
ruthless war. . . . The Communist must exert every
effort to direct . . . the development of society along
. . . the quickest way to the universal victory of the
Soviet power." [10] Together with sectarianism, sub-
jectivism, and bureaucraticism, in 1957 Mao had attacked revisionism—a vague term indicating any kind
of liberalization, moderation, or tolerance. His speech
of February 27th of that year had been, internally,
a ruse to encourage dissidents to express their views
so that they could be identified and eliminated. This
was done with gusto from the middle of 1957 on.
In 1958, Khrushchev, now solidly established in the
Soviet Union, condemned revisionism, by which, he
explained, was meant any relaxation of cultural,
economic, and political controls. He also condemned
the plurality of roads to communism, making it clear
that there was only one road. It was just the speed
at which communist parties proceeded that varied.
Soviet help, that is, military assistance, was promised
to Gomulka in the event that he should meet obstacles to ending revisionism in Poland. In the same
year, at their Ljublana congress, the Yugoslav Communist party approved Tito's motion attacking revisionism, specifically condemning bourgeois ideology
(that is, any tendency towards liberalism) and emphasizing communist ideological monopoly.

The suppression of all tendencies aimed at liberali-

[10] V. I. Lenin, *Left-Wing Communism: an Infantile Disorder*,
New York: International Publishers Co., Inc., 1934, pp. 9, 82.
Soviet here means communist, not Soviet Union.

zation was swift in the communist-controlled countries where the leadership had remained united in 1956–1957 and where tension within party ranks had been least: China, the three smaller oriental communist states, most of the Eastern European states. Suppression of revisionism took slightly longer in the Soviet Union, and several years in Hungary and Poland. In Yugoslavia, except for the persecution of Djilas (1911–   ), and his few friends, energetic measures were not taken until 1962. Although the pace varied, the process aimed at strengthening the monolithic character of the communist-controlled countries was identical. In China, besides the elimination of the unfortunates who, in 1957, had trusted Mao and had criticized the regime, there was an attempt to make the total regimentation of the population more efficient by the establishment of "communes" in 1958. In these, collective living was enforced through community kitchens, mess halls, and nurseries. They facilitated intensified party and police control. On the occasions of the celebrations for the tenth anniversary of the People's Republic and for the ninetieth anniversary of Lenin's birthday, there was a clarification of Leninism in the light of Maoism. Mao advocated a return to the Lenin of the all-out war against enemies of all kinds. He stressed the inevitability of war between capitalism and socialism. Later, the economic failures of 1959–1961 were attributed to the enemies of the regime and there was, especially in 1961, an intensification of repressive measures. The destruction of the traditional Chinese family, rigid regulation of marriages in the communes, intensive indoctrination at all levels and in all classes were followed in 1962 by the forced evacuation of about 30 million people from the cities.

Suffering was undoubtedly great in China in the

years immediately following 1957. It led to sporadic attempts at rioting or even at revolt, and to the desperate flight of tens of thousands from Tibet to India and Nepal in 1959 and from the Canton area to Hong Kong and Macao in 1962. By 1963 about one and a half million people in Hong Kong were refugees from communist China. But the dissatisfaction should not be exaggerated. Hundreds of millions of Chinese supported the regime; the dissidents were only small minorities. The hold of the party over the nation was strengthened. Anti-Mao communists were as ineffectual after 1957 as anticommunists had been after 1949.

In the Soviet Union, the 1958 episode involving the poet Pasternak was clear evidence that the "new course" was simply the return to the "old" one. At their 3d congress in 1959, Soviet writers showed that they were as docile as they had been under Stalin. Khrushchev encouraged some criticism of Stalin (including the indictment of forced labor camps by Solzhenitsyn in *One Day in the Life of Ivan Denisovich*), allowed for a while the publication of works by nonconformist poets like Tvardovsky and Yevtushenko and by the erratic critic Ehrenburg, and permitted some limited debate in literary magazines. But the issue of freedom of expression could not be raised. Painters and other artists were told in no uncertain terms not to deviate from the path of socialist realism. To the dismay of Western wishful thinkers, it had once again been made abundantly clear by 1963 that the party, not the individual, would decide what artists and writers would produce.

Antiparty Soviet communists were sent to far-off places, but not liquidated. On the other hand, executions for so-called economic crimes increased sharply, particularly in 1962–1963. This was the simple, old-

fashioned response to the problems of inefficiency and
waste. To end the flight of Soviet citizens trying to
escape to Scandinavia, stricter controls were established
on the Baltic coast. Vestiges of Jewish culture in the
western regions of the Soviet Union and of Islamic
culture in Asiatic and European areas were obliterated;
schools and places of worship were compelled to close;
there were religious motivations in the death penalties
inflicted ostensibly for economic crimes in the middle
of 1963. While paying compliments to Popes John
XXIII and Paul VI, and taking maximum advantage
of their sincere desire for peaceful coexistence, atheism
was stressed with a vigor reminiscent of the early days
of communist rule. The currency reform of 1961
amounted to a confiscation of savings; it was explained
as a further step in the progress from socialism to
communism; it increased the citizens' dependence on
the holders of political and economic power. Through
investigations and arrests, people were discouraged
from owning their homes. The poisoning by the secret
police of a defector in Vienna in 1962, the ill-treatment in the same year of British pacifists in Moscow,
the harassment of foreign diplomats, the jailing of
foreign students and of evangelical preachers, the
punishment of party members accused of nationalist
deviation all were part of the general picture of
greater repression. The post–1957 Soviet regime had
a clearer vision of needs and limits than Stalin had
ever had. There was sufficient repression to prevent
expressions of dissent, but not more. Of course, no
one knew how much of this self-control was due to
a decision taken by the dominant faction and how
much to the weakness of that same faction and the
pressure exercised by internal divisions.

The execution of Nagy, Maletar (1911–1958), and
others in 1958, closed the tragic chapter of the 1956

Hungarian revolution. The new ruler in Budapest, Kadar (1912–   ), had been imprisoned by the Stalinists, but his antirevisionism was as strong as that of his predecessor Rakosi. Fearful of a repetition of 1956 events, Kadar moved cautiously, but his goal remained the totalitarian communist society. Most concessions made to economic, religious, and intellectual groups had been withdrawn by 1963. In Poland, the dismissal of the minister of culture in 1958 heralded the advent of the campaign against revisionism. Largely because of the hold exercised over large sections of the population by a closely-knit Catholic clergy, the position of the communist minority in Poland was even more difficult than in Hungary. Gomulka moved carefully along the identical path followed by Kadar, and by the middle of 1963 he felt strong enough to revive the policy of repression of the Catholic clergy, suspended in 1956, through an attack on Catholic bishops; he also replaced soft-line communists with hard-line ones in the Politburo. Some modest grumbling and the perennial question of Slovak nationalism did not seem to affect seriously the position of Novotny in Czechoslovakia. In Bulgaria, a factional squabble erupted at the end of 1962 and was settled with the intervention of Soviet party leaders; it did not shake the regime's control over the population. Playing his own game in the Soviet-Chinese rift, the Rumanian dictator Gheorghiu-Dej tried in 1963 to assert his autonomy vis-à-vis the Soviet Union, but this instead seemed to strengthen the hold of the party over the Rumanian nation.

Events in East Germany showed how close the "new course" was to the old one. The border between East and West Germany was controlled more efficiently than ever, and illegal crossings of East German refugees became rarer. A wall erected in August 1961 through

the city of Berlin sealed the hatch that many of the
nearly 3 million people fleeing from East Germany
had passed through. (They represented one sixth of
the population of the German Democratic Republic.)
Killings and kidnappings occurred repeatedly along
the Berlin wall and the East German border. There
was no relaxation of the tension caused by the communist decision to achieve control over the whole
of Berlin. Repression in East Germany and elsewhere
was part of the return to Leninist orthodoxy.

Antirevisionism in Yugoslavia remained more verbal
than actual for several years. Within limits, however,
it functioned. The events of November 1956 in Hungary made Tito suspicious of some of his collaborators.
There was no pro-Sovietism among the Yugoslav population, but friends of the Soviet existed among party
members. A genuine revisionist was M. Djilas. His
ill-treatment at the hands of Tito received considerable
publicity, and his books helped many to understand
the nature of communism more correctly. Arrests of
Croat nationalists in 1957 were followed by arrests
of socialists in 1958 and of Catholics in 1960. The
flow of Yugoslav exiles crossing the Adriatic to Italy,
or the Alps to Austria, never stopped. All the same,
life was more tolerable in those years in Yugoslavia
than in other communist-controlled countries. This
did not imply an essential difference between Titoist
and other interpretations of Marxism-Leninism. It
mainly implied less governmental and party efficiency.
To strengthen his position, Tito had himself proclaimed Life-President of Yugoslavia in 1963.

Cultural exchanges between states of the Soviet bloc
and foreign noncommunist countries increased. More
foreigners from capitalistic and neutralist countries
visited the Soviet Union. Rigid control continued to
be exercised over tourist travel. The increase was more

a sign of communist success than of liberalization. By the early 1960s, at least in the Soviet Union, a generation had grown up which generally accepted communism as wholeheartedly as English-speaking nations accept democracy. It was a mistake to interpret grumbling against one or another aspect of communist life as a sign of opposition. There was no abandoning of coercion; there was less need to use it. Only carefully screened and foolproof communists were allowed to go abroad—as participants in international gatherings, as students, as tourists. Whatever the status, they were always official representatives and spokesmen for communism: they never brought back a new idea to the Soviet Union or the satellites. Those who defected from the satellites were noncommunists before going abroad. Western visitors to communist countries enjoyed freedom of movement only where the inhabitants of visited regions were loyal communists.

The modern Western concept of education as a means to the emancipation of the individual is alien to communist ideology. In the more recent period communists continued to stress, and rendered more efficient in the countries they controlled, monopoly over schools and all media of communication. The aim was to achieve total conformity through indoctrination. Knowing that an illiterate is often freer in his thinking than an indoctrinated literate and that skills increase in the measure in which people are vocationally instructed, communists made great efforts to achieve universal literacy and to promote vocational instruction. These efforts were successful. Intensive indoctrination carried through with efficient educational and psychological techniques increased the hold of the party over the population. At the same time a large, competent labor force was developed.

In the Soviet Union and in the advanced European

satellites, communist leaders (acting pragmatically
even if in so doing they contradicted their own ideology) left a maximum of freedom of inquiry and discussion to physicists and chemists (while scientists in
other fields were strictly controlled). Ample funds for
research and experimentation in the fields considered
militarily and strategically the most important were
made available. The outcome was greater scientific
knowledge, advancement in technology, and spectacular successes, which increased communist prestige considerably. The impact of Sputnik (1957), Lunik (1959),
cosmonauts' flights since 1961—particularly in the nations of underdeveloped areas—should not be minimized. Thanks again to scientific knowledge, technological inventions, and large capital investment, communist-controlled countries advanced rapidly in the
field of military preparedness.

For ideological, political, and military reasons, rapid
economic growth was a main concern in each center
of communist power. Khrushchev's faction had advocated the absolute priority of heavy industry over
lighter consumer industries and over agriculture.
Communist propagandists stress only achievement,
their opponents stress only the failures. There were
both: "The Soviet Union has in the period since
World War II succeeded systematically in its long-
range targets for heavy industry. . . . In 1946 Stalin
announced targets for the period 1960–1965: steel, 60
million tons; coal, 500 million tons; petroleum, 60
million. . . . In 1960 the USSR actually produced . . . 65
million tons of steel, 513 million of coal, 148 million
of petroleum." [11] In agriculture, on the other hand,
production failed to keep up with the increase of

[11] T. P. Whitney, ed., *The Communist Blueprint for the
Future,* New York: E. P. Dutton & Co., Inc., 1962, p. xxxi.

population. There was also a constant shortage of consumer goods and of dwellings. The increase in production profited the Soviet state, that is, its political, administrative and military bureaucracy. The state became stronger, internally and externally. The benefits accruing to the Soviet people in the form of a higher standard of living were modest.

The reorganization of the Soviet economic structure effected by Khrushchev in 1957 lasted only five years. It had been based largely on the principle of vertical, or functional, decentralization (or decentralization by branches of economic activity, not by geographical areas). To this reorganization communist economists attributed, in particular, the success achieved in space exploration and in the development of intercontinental missiles. Real progress had been achieved in these and other branches of production. On the other hand, there was considerable evidence that in spite of enthusiastic official reports, economic ills had been accumulating. They were due to bureaucratic waste, duplication, uneven development, low yields in agriculture, poor quality of many manufactured goods, low level of productivity, general inefficiency.

The workers' enthusiasm of the early 1930s was no longer in evidence thirty years later. Managerial dynamism was being replaced by bureaucratic complacency. In 1962 there were reports of strikes and rioting in mining and industrial communities—chiefly the result of poor living conditions. Employees at all levels tended to move to the few metropolitan areas in the European section of the country where life was not drab as in the average Soviet city. In November 1962, bureaucratic waste alone in that year was officially estimated to have cost the equivalent of over $2 billion. Military expenses, absorbing as much as one fifth of the GNP, space exploration, and aid to foreign countries imposed a severe strain on the Soviet economy. Commitments abroad in the form of manufactured goods and machinery could not be kept. Rising prices in the summer of 1962 had cut real wages. The program to eliminate taxes on personal incomes had been suspended.

The economic structural scheme put into effect early in 1963 aimed at greater managerial autonomy, accompanied by a tightening of party controls. It was a new application of the formula once tried by Lenin: limited economic decentralization balanced by political centralization. The number of large functional and territorial trusts was reduced by about half. Each trust was granted considerable autonomy. A dual system was tried in which agriculture was made organizationally independent of industry. Different policies were applied to these two main sectors of the economy. Within industry, a sharp organizational difference was established between heavy and light industry. The use of incentives adopted from capitalistic economies was encouraged. The State Planning Committee was abolished after nearly forty years of existence, and was replaced by a Council of the National Economy, headed first by V. E. Dymshits and later by the former head of the Soviet arms industry, D. F. Ustinov. Party functions related to the economy were put under the control of A. N. Shelepin, a former secret police chief. A few Soviet economists had suggested moving toward a market economy in which costs and prices would find their natural level, but the advice was not heeded. The Soviet structural reorganization was a signal for the adoption of similar measures in the satellites. It was applauded by Tito, who had tried something similar in Yugoslavia, with little success. It was criticized by former Stalinists and by Maoists. When the scheme was put into effect, it was doubtful that an institutional reshuffling would be sufficient to cure the ills collectivism was facing as it matured.

Economic experiences in the six European satellites, in Yugoslavia, and in Albania varied. Czechoslovakia was the show place of collectivism. It had been a highly developed industrial nation during the years of independence, 1918–1939. Capital and skilled labor were more abundant than in the other satellites. Czech goods were exported widely, on both sides of the Iron Curtain. Among communist-controlled states, Czechoslovakia played an important role in the field of economic and military aid to underdeveloped countries. Minor roles were played by East Germany and Poland, and among the nonsatellites by Yugoslavia. In general, the four Balkan communist-controlled states, satellites and nonsatellites, fared less well economically than the Soviet Union and the industrially more advanced northern satellites. In 1962 the rate of industrial expansion in Yugoslavia was less than three fifths of the Soviet rate. What economic progress had been achieved was largely the result of American subsidies, which amounted to nearly $3.5 billion in fifteen years.

According to official statistics, the rate of economic growth in Czechoslovakia 1953–1961 was about the same as that of West Germany. The Polish rate of economic growth was comparable to Austria's; that of Hungary was lower than the Italian rate. Standards of living had been at approximately the same level in West and East Germany when they were both included in the German Reich: in the early 1960s real personal incomes (including social benefits) in East Germany were about two thirds of what they were in West Germany.

In China, the second five-year plan started with great fanfare. In 1958, "communes" were replacing family life, and traditional communities were being disrupted. That was also the year of "the great leap forward" in industry and agriculture, and of total mobilization of the immense Chinese labor force. Glowing accounts of astounding successes were soon circulated: they proved to be as false as official Soviet reports of the 1930s. In 1959 what private ownership in farming remained was abolished. Bad crops led to a debacle in agriculture in 1960, with famine and near-famine conditions in many parts of China. In some areas a person's diet averaged barely 600 calories per day; in vast regions it was no more than 1200. Labor efficiency declined and there was greater incidence of cholera in the south. Better crops in 1963 seemed to improve the situation. Mining, however, continued to expand, particularly coal and iron. New power plants increased the output of energy. Besides agriculture, the gap between planned goals and results was especially great in manufacturing. In 1962 steel production was estimated at about 8–10 million tons, half of what had been planned. In part, difficulties were due to the decision of the communist leaders to strengthen military forces and, with Chinese financial aid, to increase communist pressure in countries near and far. On the basis of unofficial estimates, in 1963 the per capita average income in China, about $70, was inferior to that of India, which, prior to the communist take over in China in 1949, was supposed to have a lower standard of living than the Chinese one.

Since the establishment of the Chinese People's Republic, Soviet economic contributions to China had amounted to billions of dollars. Soviet technicians had set up factories in Manchuria and in China proper. In 1960 came the withdrawal of many technicians, but economic aid continued. In 1962 the Chinese leaders criticized the Soviet intention to reorganize the economy along lines of decentralization. This was Titoist revisionism. Soviet emphasis on incentives also met with criticism: Chinese communists stressed instead the policy of equalization of incomes. However, failures imposed a reshuffle of economic institutions in China: ambitious plans were abandoned, peasants were allowed to leave the "communes," industrial managers were given some autonomy. At the end of 1962 it was announced that the industrialization of China would take longer than originally planned. After the crisis of the summer of 1963 in Soviet-Chinese relations, the likelihood of further Soviet aid to the Chinese economy had become remote.

Along with India, Egypt, Mexico, and many other countries, China saw a rapid increase in the population. Chinese communists were baffled by the population problem. It is denied by Marxist-Leninist theory, which postulates the unlimited capacity of a collectivist economy to satisfy all wants, regardless of the size of the population. But the problem existed. At first it was ignored by the newly-established regime. Then, in the middle fifties, came a short period during which Maoists seemingly made their own neo-Malthusian theories and advocated the practice of birth control. After the clarification of the Chinese communist line in 1957–1958, the population problem was once again ignored, as being contrary to the principles of Marxism-Leninism. Then a new reversal occurred in 1963 when birth control was again encouraged, abortions were allowed, and contraceptives were made available to the masses.

In the tenth year after Stalin's death the fourteen communist-controlled states (including Cuba), with a total population of over 1 billion people, had gross national products inferior to those of the sixteen European democracies, with 270 million people, and altogether about half those of the United States and Canada (210 million people). The vaunted superiority of collectivism over all other economic systems—in the name of which revolutions had been made, wars had been waged, millions of people had been killed, and tens of millions uprooted—still lacked evidence.

The New Course: Polycentrism or Pluralism?

Within each section of the communist movement the new course did not vary essentially from the old one. But in the relationships between communist-controlled states and between communist parties, the new course differed more and more after 1958 from that maintained until 1957. One development overshadowed all others: the unity of the communist movement, held steadfastly for several decades against all centrifugal forces, was in jeopardy.

Differences between communists concerned neither fundamental principles nor goals, but means: policies, and the pace at which they were to be pursued. These differences, however, were enough to cause severe tension. There was probably as much disagreement on policies and pace in the twenty-one-nation NATO-SEATO-CENTO bloc as in the fourteen-nation communist bloc. But among Americans, French, Turks, Thais, Australians, willingness to compromise, even if at times severely limited, was taken for granted, and discussion usually led to a measure of accord, sufficient at least to maintain the cohesion of the bloc. Among communists, stress on unity was greater but opposition to compromise was part of the ideology, and discussions often led to bitter antagonism. Dogmatism had made communists strong against their opponents: now it was weakening communism by making agreement on controversial issues difficult, at times impossible.

Personal rivalries and power politics had their share in straining relationships between autonomous centers of communist power. There were also serious dissensions on internal policies (for instance, concerning the degree of collectivization in agriculture, the degree of centralization in industrial enterprises, the treatment of dissident and unassimilable groups), and—more important—on external policies (the degree of coexistence with capitalism, the range of brinkmanship, cooperation in underdeveloped areas with middle-class nationalists and non-Marxist socialists). Dissensions degenerated into bitter enmities. At the time of the Moscow ideological debate, held in the summer of 1963, the gulf between Khruschevites and Maoists (or between Soviet and Chinese communists) had become deeper than that between Stalinists and Titoists fifteen years earlier, nearly as deep as the one between Stalinists and Trotskyites thirty-five years earlier. Trotsky had been destroyed and Tito had never amounted to much ideologically or politically, but China was on a par with the Soviet Union because of its sheer size, its military preparedness, and the dynamism of Chinese communists. The unitarian character of the movement, which had been a main source of strength before and after 1917, was seriously impaired—possibly even gone. It is true that in spite of the depth of the gulf there were no excommunications as there had been in 1948 and in 1927, that in spite of the differences communists continued to consider themselves members of one family, but it could be expected that in due course the new situation would affect the appeal of communism to its most effective supporters, the radical members of the intelligentsia.

The process leading to the weakening of the uni-

tarian character of communism was rather slow in
achieving impetus. At first, in the years immediately
following the 1956–1957 crises, efforts were made to
maintain unity and cooperation among communist-
controlled states, and among communists everywhere.
Unity matters ideologically not less than practically
to Marxist-Leninists, who like to contrast the cohesion
of a communist society with the divisions characterizing
free democracies. As a gesture of friendship toward
Tito, the Cominform had been abolished in 1956, and
the publication through which the party line was announced had ceased to exist. New authoritative world-
wide communist publications were the *Marxist World
Review* and *Problems of Peace and Socialism*. Opportunities for announcing general directives and policies
were provided by frequent meetings, in which the
leaders of all communist parties participated. Of these
parties there were 88 in 1963. The definition of communism drafted by the Soviet leaders [12] was accepted
by all parties. It reasserted the Marxist-Leninist foundation of communism. It also stressed once again faith
in the vision of an earthly paradise, which for tens
of millions of loyal communists is more important than
disputes about the interpretation of Marxist-Leninist
principles.

Particularly important was a December 1960 conference at which agreement was reached on four propo-

[12] The definition is the following: "Communism is a classless
society with one form of public ownership of the means of
production and full social equality of all members of society;
under it, the all-round development of people will be accompanied by the growth of productive forces through continuous
progress in science and technology, all sources of public wealth
will gush forth abundantly, and the great principle 'from each
according to his ability, to each according to his needs' will
be implemented."

sitions: war was not inevitable; the United States, as the leading "imperialist" nation, was the chief enemy; communist parties were organizationally autonomous; communists everywhere must be concerned first and foremost with the unity of the communist movement. Congresses of the communist parties were used as channels through which dissensions would be aired and modifications of the party line made public. In spite of disagreements and mutual accusations of disloyalty to Marxism-Leninism, cooperation between communist-controlled states continued during the first years of polycentrism, in the financial and economic fields. The 1925–1927 break between Stalinism and Trotskyism had been total. The 1948 break between the Soviet Union and Tito had led to a communist quarantine of Yugoslavia and the execution or expulsion of Titoists everywhere. After 1958, whatever the verbal exchanges, trade continued between the Soviet Union and China, as did, for a while, Soviet subsidies and grants to China. For a number of years anti-Soviet Albania maintained communications with several Soviet satellites. North Korea and North Vietnam, although leaning more and more toward Maoism, continued to receive Soviet aid. On a world level, the more prosperous communist parties subsidized less prosperous ones. Close connection was maintained with the underground communist parties (for instance, by the French Communist party with the Iberian ones, by the CPSU with the parties in Arab countries, by the Indian Communist party with the Pakistani one). Khrushchevites, Maoists, and Titoists worked together in Algeria, Cameroon, the Congo, Guinea, Somalia, Cuba and other areas not included in the sphere of influence of a specific party or dictatorship.

Close cooperation between communist-controlled

states was evident in the United Nations. Whatever the problem facing the Assembly, the Security Council and other councils, and the thirteen United Nations agencies, communist member-states functioned (with few exceptions) as a unit. There were instances in which Yugoslavia adopted a position different from that of the USSR, but not many.

As long as Stalin was alive, communists acted as if their main purpose was to prevent the United Nations from fulfilling its functions. Their obstructionist tactics were similar to those adopted in the immediate postwar period in coalition governments of democratic countries. After Stalin's death the emphasis shifted: the aim was now to exploit to the full the opportunities offered by the world organization and its agencies for spreading communist influence. This was a revival of the unsuccessful attempt made in the 1930s with the League of Nations. There was also evidence of a long-range goal: to achieve control of the United Nations itself. Communist tactics consisted mainly of two sets of measures. One concerned the structural reorganization of the United Nations in such a way as to give a preponderant voice to the minority communist group. A three-man committee would replace the Secretary General of the UN Secretariat. The development of an international civil service and of an international police force loyal to the United Nations, not to member-states, was opposed. The other measure aimed at forming within the United Nations a solid fellow-traveling bloc of neutral or uncommitted nations that would consistently support communist policies. Unity among democratic member-states and their friends, diplomatic skill, and firmness were required to check communist efforts to subvert the United Nations and make it an instrument of communist expansion.

With the exception of isolated, small, and recalcitrant Albania, integration between European communist states remained close in the early sixties. The Soviet bloc—including (besides the Soviet Union) Bulgaria, Czechoslovakia, East Germany, Hungary, Poland, and Rumania, and in Asia, Mongolia—was a functional reality. (Since 1961, Cuba was also considered a member of the bloc.) Whatever may have been the exact nature of the relationships between parties and factions led by Khrushchev, Zhivkov, Novotny, Ulbricht, Kadar, Gomulka, Gheorghiu-Dej, and Tsedenbal, the Comecon did function, cooperation between the eight member-states increased, common projects were carried out. Just as the Common Market may one day render secondary the political boundaries between its members, the same is likely to happen with the Comecon. The Eastern Security Treaty (or Warsaw Pact) produced between the USSR and the satellites a more closely integrated military community than the North Atlantic Treaty. The thirty Soviet divisions in Eastern Europe remained the strongest guarantee that there would be no repetition of the events of 1953 and 1956.

Closer integration of European communist-controlled states in the early sixties included Yugoslavia. The rift between Soviet and Titoist communism had been slow in healing. The treatment inflicted on dissident Hungarian communists after the failure of the 1956 revolution had brought Soviet-Yugoslav relations to a low point. Soviet credits to Yugoslavia had been cancelled in 1958. Visits of prominent communists from the satellites to Belgrade had not improved the situation. It was the period when Tito saw himself as a major spokesman for uncommitted nations, a leader whose influence would be felt from central America to southeastern Asia, perhaps the arbiter in the conflict between the USA and the USSR. A change in Soviet-Yugoslav relations became perceptible in 1960. Closer contacts were established later by Yugoslavia with the Soviet Union, Comecon, and the Eastern Security Treaty Organization. A friendly speech by Khrushchev in May 1962, Tito's visit to Moscow in November of that year, and Khrushchev's return visit to Belgrade in 1963 put the seal on reconciliation, for the time being. After a fourteen-year schism, Titoism seemed to be gradually reabsorbed into the mainstream of Marxism-Leninism, as interpreted by Soviet communists.

In the relations between Khrushchevism and Maoism, which is to say between the Soviet Union and China, polycentrism neutralized the efforts to maintain unity and cooperation. There were disagreements about the pace of pursuing goals: collectivization, industrialization, ideological conformism, elimination of unassimilable groups. There were economic elements of friction in relation to trade, financing, exploitation, and allocation of scarce resources. Another source of friction concerned the attitude to be adopted toward bourgeois (noncommunist and nonsocialist) revolutionaries in the underdeveloped areas of the world. However, the main factors in the Sino-Soviet disputes were two, related to each other: the policy to be adopted in relation to "capitalist" countries (the United States and its allies); and the speed with which communists should try to take over in countries of interest either to the Soviet Union or China, in which communism had a sufficient popular base.

In connection with the second factor, the border between West Pakistan and India represents roughly the dividing line between Soviet and Chinese areas of expansion. For several decades a main Soviet target had been central and western Europe. After the end of 1952 this was no longer the case, and the main targets were the eastern Mediterranean and the Middle East. The Chinese line of expansion was southeastern Asia, with India as one wing and Australasia as another. Beyond what may be called the Soviet and Chinese spheres of influence were areas of Africa and of Latin America in which communism was growing. What should be done, by the Chinese in South Korea, South Vietnam, Laos, and Burma, by the Soviets in Iran, Iraq, and Greece, by both in Algeria, the Congo, Brazil, Venezuela? Thinking of communism as a whole —as communists do—one realizes the importance of policies adopted by leaders of world communism. In the period immediately following 1957, decisions of the Chinese Presidium counted as much as those of the Soviet Presidium.

Any decision had to take the United States into account. Americans were present in South Vietnam and in Iran, even if simply as advisers and instructors. The American 7th Fleet patrolled the China sea and the 6th Fleet patrolled the Mediterranean. America protected Formosa and Turkey. There were American military bases in the Middle East and in southeastern Asia. Americans could not remain indifferent to what happened in Latin America. Discussions among communist leaders always turned to the fundamental problem of policy toward the United States.

Soviet leaders favored coexistence. In Moscow this term never meant what it did in democratic nations. It meant a policy of maximum pressure against "capitalism" and "imperialism," short of war. Chinese leaders were less deterred by the risk of war. Again, the difference was only one of degree: nevertheless it was important enough to cause great bitterness and tension, and it had a number of causes. China bordered on weak states on many sides, but the Soviet Union adjoined, both in Europe and the Middle East, states that could rely on immediate American aid. Some even possessed defensive capacities of their own. The buffer states between NATO-CENTO and the Soviet Union presented greater obstacles than the buffer states between SEATO and China. Rulers of a nuclear power, Soviet leaders were more aware than the Chinese of what a nuclear war would mean, and of American nuclear preparedness. In the early sixties, China was still in a Stalinist phase of development, while Stalinism was looked upon with distaste, officially, in the USSR. After 1957 the communist leadership exercised a more absolute control over China than the Khrushchevites exercised in the Soviet Union. Being poorer, China had less to lose in a conflict than the Soviet Union. More populous, China could easily afford large human losses. However much or little the various factors counted, a rift there was.

Two simultaneous crises in the autumn of 1962 brought the tension between Soviet and Chinese communist leaders to a head. The Soviet Union had been setting up military bases in Cuba, and China had been mounting an attack against India in Tibet. No one in the West knew at the time if the two parallel initiatives had been taken independently or as a result of prior consultation between Moscow and Peiping. The Soviet leaders, however, miscalculated American reactions (as the Japanese had done in 1941 and the Germans in 1917). Fearful of the American blockade of Cuba, Khrushchev and his colleagues decided on at least a temporary partial withdrawal. During the same movement. However, tension became greater early territory with little or no opposition. Unable to count on Soviet support and fearful of mounting American and British aid to India, the Chinese stopped their invasion and withdrew. The leaders in Peiping saw in the Soviet vacillations a betrayal of communism and an inability to live up to Leninist teachings. The leaders in Moscow accused the Chinese of irresponsibility and of damaging the communist cause in the neutral and uncommitted nations. Tito's visit to Moscow was interpreted in Peiping as a concession to the hated revisionism. Peiping's anti-Titoism and support of Stalinist Albania led Khrushchevites to accuse the Chinese of dogmatism. With different names, it was the old internal conflict that Lenin and Stalin had once dealt with. This time, of course, there was a difference: both left-wing and right-wing deviationists had military power of their own. In the event of a showdown, Maoists could mobilize the manpower and economic resources of China and her friends, just as Tito could mobilize those of Yugoslavia. They were not impotent, as Trotsky and Bukharin had been a few decades earlier.

A restraining influence was exercised, for a while at least, by the fear that an intracommunist armed clash would bring about a repetition—either in Europe or in Asia—of the events of 1956, by a shared hatred for the United States and other democracies, and by a meagerness of economic resources. Words sounded louder than deeds. Early in 1963, the Sino-Soviet rift had not yet reached the proportions of absolute incompatibility which had characterized the schisms of 1925–1927 and of 1948. Khrushchevites and Maoists participated in the same meetings, were still on speaking terms in the countries not controlled by communists, and considered each other as members of the same movement. However tension became greater early in the summer. July 5th had been decided upon as the date for an ideological debate between Chinese and Soviet communists. Three weeks earlier, on June 14th, the Central Committee of the Chinese Communist

party sent a long letter to its counterpart in Moscow
stating its position on controversial issues—which
boiled down to one point only, a request for greater
aggressiveness. Soviet authorities forbade the diffusion
of the letter in the areas they controlled and replied
early in July with their own counterstatement. The
ideological debate opened on the appointed day, the
Chinese delegation being led by Teng Hsaio-ping and
the Soviet by M. A. Suslov; there was no dialogue
between the delegations but only a series of mono-
logues. The meeting was suspended on July 20th.
Again, there was not for the time being a complete
schism, and each side continued to refer to the other
as comrades. But national communist parties were
taking sides; minority factions appeared within the
parties, challenging the leadership; fronts like the
International Democratic Women's Federation, the
International Federation of Democratic Youth and that
of Trade Unions, the World Peace Council, the Afri-
can-Asian People's Solidarity Organization, became
split. Polycentrism was fathering a new situation:
pluralism.

The Maoist or Chinese ideological formulation was
considerably clearer than that of Titoism fifteen years
earlier, much clearer than that of Trotskyism. In the
name of a correct interpretation of Leninism, Maoists
condemned peaceful coexistence with "capitalism,"
alliances with middle-class revolutionaries, the creation
of autonomous centers of power in the economy, in-
equality of incomes, and other "capitalistic" incentives.
By the middle of 1963, the party leaders of Albania,
North Korea, and North Vietnam had sided with the
Maoists (although the Vietnamese Ho Chi Minh, in
collaboration with others, had tried to bring about
an agreement between Chinese and Soviet communists).

Siding with China also were the leaders of most other Asian communist parties, including that of Indonesia, the largest party outside communist-controlled states. There were, usually underground, pro-Chinese factions in European and Latin American parties controlled by Khrushchevites. In Asia, Mongolian and most Indian party leaders sided with the Soviet Union. The Cuban Castro seemed to lean toward the Chinese at the end of 1962; after a lengthy visit to the Soviet Union in 1963 he came out strongly in favor of the Soviet position.

The dispute between Moscow and Peiping did not noticeably weaken the position of the communists in the countries they controlled. From this point of view, the impact was less than that of Titoism in 1948. What the leaders decided was accepted by the rank and file and imposed on the rest of the population. The dispute did, however, affect communism elsewhere to some extent. Party members and would-be communists were faced with the problem of having to choose between Khrushchevites and Maoists—between two different policies. Often a two-headed movement has less power of attraction than a unified one.

Disputes did not at first moderate communist aggressiveness. The Cuban and Indian ventures of 1962 had not been isolated episodes. Whatever the tensions within the communist movement, the post–1957 polycentric situation did not weaken efforts to act according to Lenin's principle that "as long as capitalism exists, we cannot live in peace . . . concessions are a continuation of war." Tactics changed; some thought infiltration preferable to overt attacks; some wanted to go faster than others; but the over-all communist goals remained the same. While talking vehemently of peace (as Lenin had done in 1917), all available pressure short of actual major military operations was brought to bear against democratic countries—particularly, of course, the United States.

The relative lull in the aggressiveness of communist-controlled states after the Korean armistice of 1953 and the Indochinese agreements of 1954, had ended in 1958. A dangerous situation developed in that year in the Strait of Formosa, as the result of intensive shelling by Chinese communists of the nationalist-held offshore islands of Matsu and Quemoy. (Nearly half a million rounds of ammunition were fired against the two islands between August 23d and October 24th.) There was a flare-up of the continuing German and Berlin crisis when, on November 10th, Khrushchev issued a statement amounting to an ultimatum. Americans ignored the ultimatum, while the British pressed once again for a Summit meeting. There were exchanges of visits of Soviet and American dignitaries in June 1959; Khrushchev was invited to visit the United States, and a short-lived "spirit of Camp David" renewed the illusions linked to the 1955 "spirit of Geneva." The year 1959 witnessed the end of Tibetan autonomy, the occupation of about 12,000 square miles of Indian territory by the Chinese, who claimed a total of 50,000 square miles in the Himalayan ranges, and increased activity of Soviet- and Chinese-supplied guerrillas in Laos. Large-scale massacres were carried out in the spring of 1959 by communists at Kirkuk in Iraq, where, during the dictatorial rule of General Kassem (1958–1963), communists had a freer hand than in any other Arab state.

In 1960, the capture of a high altitude American reconnaissance plane over Soviet territory provided communists everywhere with a pretext for a renewed propaganda onslaught against the United States. The patiently arranged Summit meeting of May 1960 in

Paris was a total failure. Prodded, very likely, by the Maoist leaders, Khrushchev acted in September at the Assembly of the United Nations as if the word co-existence, even in the limited communist meaning, had never been pronounced. High-powered communist agents appeared in Cuba, the Congo, Algeria. Tensions were building up—to the great satisfaction of most communists. Communist aggressiveness in 1961 included these high points: the building of the Berlin wall in August; the Soviet resumption, soon after, of nuclear tests following a thirty-four-month suspension; threats to Finland coupled with advice to end parliamentarianism and democratic procedure; the undermining of the United Nations' peace-making efforts in the Congo, and virulent attacks against the then Secretary-general of the UN.

In 1962 warning threats were uttered by Soviet leaders against the German Federal Republic and against neutrals contemplating association with the Common Market, particularly Austria and Sweden. Threats were made by Chinese leaders against the Himalayan state of Bhutan and Sikkim. Added stress was laid in all countries of the Warsaw Treaty Organization, and in China, on military preparedness. Contrary to the agreement concerning the neutralization of Laos, foreign communist guerrillas, estimated at several tens of thousands, stayed in the country. Killings and kidnappings on the borders of Berlin and of West Germany increased. Soviet airplanes and missiles, and an unspecified number of troops were sent to Cuba during the summer and early autumn. In October, Chinese troops invaded, from Tibet, Ladakh, and the northeastern frontier area, both belonging to India. After a partial withdrawal, Chinese troops remained in occupation of large mountainous Indian territories. American pressure forced a partial Soviet military withdrawal from Cuba, but the island remained a Soviet political satellite. Chinese communists, particularly, spurred the Indonesian government to military action in West Irian in 1962, to support of an insurrection in Brunei, and to opposition to the newly-established Malaysian Federation in 1963. Chinese and Soviet communists were both behind the intensification of guerrilla warfare in South Vietnam and its resumption in Laos in 1963. The cold war was waged as effectively from 1958 on as it had been when Stalin ruled, and at times it became fairly hot. To complete the picture, it is necessary to add that Soviet, satellite, Chinese, and Yugoslav communists acted as a well-coordinated team in their efforts to achieve as much influence as possible in the underdeveloped areas of the world.

In most advanced democratic countries, communists continued for a while to lose ground after the events of 1956–1957. At the end of 1962 there were about 2½ million party members in twenty-six states of Europe, the Americas, Asia, and Australasia, described by the communists as "developed capitalist countries." Of that total, more than 2 million were in Italy and France—a considerable decline from the more than 3 million of the immediate postwar period. In European democratic states, the number of votes received at general elections by communist candidates had reached over 16 million after the war ended. A decade and a half later, in considerably larger electorates, the vote was down to about 13 million. Among the English-speaking members of the Commonwealth and in the United States, party membership had become negligible and the activity of remaining party members had also declined considerably. Measures like the heavy fines imposed by a federal court on party officials for failure to register as foreign agents further discouraged communist activity in the United States. In these twenty-six countries, the decline of communist parties had been fairly general from 1946–1962. (Practically the only exception had been the electoral success in Italy in 1953.) But in 1963 there were signs of communist revival in some countries. Communists still commanded the allegiance of large sections of the intelligentsia and of the wage earners in Finland, Greece, Iceland, Israel, and Japan as well as in Italy and France; communists gained votes in the national elections in France in November 1962 and in Italy in April 1963; communist undergrounds seemed to be gaining adherents both in Greece and in the Iberian states. Gaullism was driving many Frenchmen to the side of the communists; the fear of clericalism in Italy and of rightist authoritarianism in other Mediterranean countries had the same effect. Where they were still strong, communists seemed to be aiming at the reestablishment of popular fronts along the pattern of the 1930s.

In the early sixties, communism—polycentric or pluralistic—gained ground in the underdeveloped areas of Africa, Asia, and Latin America. There, forty-nine communist parties had seen their membership climb to nearly 3 million by the beginning of 1963. In these areas new situations had been created by developments unrelated to communism: decolonization in Africa and Asia, the appeal exercised by *Fidelismo* in many parts of Latin America. Communists were hard at work to turn these situations to their advantage.

The movement for independence in former colonial dependencies suddenly accelerated. The exhaustion resulting from World War II and the temporary occupation of enemy overseas possessions by the Germans, Japanese, and their allies were contributing causes. So, too, were the strength of the opposition in Euro-

pean mother countries immediately after the war of
movements (democratic socialism, for instance) to all
forms of colonialism, and the realization that colonies
were economic as well as political liabilities, not assets
as previously claimed. To these factors were added
American pressure and local nationalist agitation.
Decolonization in underdeveloped areas had actually
begun in 1922 with the recognition of the independence of Egypt. By 1945 six former dependencies
had become independent and fourteen more were
added in 1947–1956. Beginning in 1957, gradualness
gave way to abruptness. In less than seven years thirty
independent states came into existence and ten more
reached the threshold of independence. In most cases
power was in the hands of small groups of intellectuals
or of the military. The prevailing mood among the
new leaders was emotional and extremist. Most of
them thought of themselves as national socialists and
were strongly anti-Western.

Except in some of the countries of southeastern
Asia, the communists did not try to take over in the
former colonial areas: their main concern was the
establishment of friendly regimes that would not
obstruct the communists' efforts to strengthen their
organization. With lavish receptions, economic aid,
the sending of technicians (who were also propagandists), and students' scholarships, the rulers of communist-controlled countries made efforts to win over
the leaders of the newly independent countries. By 1962
the equivalent of $4 billion had been granted in
aid: not much in comparison with the $35 billion
given by the Americans and British, but highly publicized. Twelve thousand young people from these
countries had been trained in Soviet or satellite vocational institutes; 8500 Soviet technicians had been
sent out. In mid–1962 about 3000 young Africans

were studying in communist universities and the same number of Soviet and satellite technicians were in Africa; 2500 young Cubans were students in Soviet and satellite universities and technical institutes. Among their successes, communists counted the dependence of the Indonesian nationalists on the Indonesian Communist Party, the doubling of the communist vote in India at the 1962 elections, the triumph in Algeria of the faction of Moslem nationalists that had received Chinese support. There had been setbacks, instead, in the Congo, where the UN-supported central government eliminated a procommunist regional government early in 1962; in Guinea, where the dominant national socialists at one point expelled Soviet advisers and technicians; and also in Iraq, where an anticommunist dictatorship replaced the procommunist one early in 1963.

The victory of Fidel Castro's 26th of July Movement in Cuba early in January 1959 had vast repercussions in Latin America, where communism (except in a few cases) had remained limited mostly to not very efficient groups of the intelligentsia. The *Fidelista* demagogic direct democracy, their *caudillismo,* confused agrarianism, deep emotionalism, and general political vagueness did not appeal to the communists. But *Fidelismo* had a mass appeal and could become a mass movement: properly exploited, it could lead communists to success. For historically-minded communists, *Fidelistas*—the Latin American version of agrarian socialists—could play in parts of Latin America the role other agrarian socialists, the Left Revolutionary Socialists, had played in Russia in 1917–1918 and the *jacquerie* in China in 1947–1949. In February 1960 Mikoyan visited Cuba. Within two years Cuba had become the fourteenth communist-controlled state in the world, the first in the Western Hemisphere.

Communists were in key positions in Cuba; Castro had declared Cuba a socialist state and himself a Marxist-Leninist, 80 percent of Cuban trade was with the countries of the communist bloc; thousands of Cuban students attended Soviet and Czech universities; hundreds of young Cuban officers were trained in Soviet military academies. Cuba had become a major communist base, politically and militarily. It remained a major base even after the crisis of October-November 1962. Cuba sided with the USSR in the 1963 dispute between Soviet and Chinese communists, but kept on good terms with China. Outside Cuba, communists (without in any way relinquishing their own organization) became enthusiastic spokesmen for *Fidelismo*. The tortuous relationships maintained for years with the radical rightist dictators, with Perón, Vargas, and Batista, even with Perez Jimenez in Venezuela, were now replaced by all-out infiltration of *Fidelismo*. The main target remained Latin American democratic forces; the main enemies, besides the United States, were the movements and parties led by Betancourt, Bosch, De La Torre, Figueres, Illia. In 1963, a large-scale terrorist *Fidelista*-communist campaign was under way in Venezuela and in Columbia.

By the beginning of 1963 there were nearly 42 million card-carrying communists in the world. Communist dictatorships ruled two thirds of the Eurasian continent and had a foothold in the Western Hemisphere. Communism had come a long way since two dozen followers had rallied round Lenin in 1903.

CHAPTER ... 4

Conclusion

What Next?

In attempting to answer the question "what next?" it is necessary to keep in mind what communists believe in, what their aspirations are, how they interpret the world in which we live. Communists are moved by the consciousness and horror of economic suffering, by a sincere desire to end the exploitation of man by man, and by the conviction that only collectivism can lead to affluence. They believe that material abundance will dispose of the problems and difficulties confronting mankind and that all means leading to the triumph of their movement are legitimate. Their interpretation of man, and the absolute nature of their beliefs, oblige communists to enforce political despotism. Everything that communists are doing has already been tried, at times successfully, by other movements. What is new is the ability, supplied by technological progress, to exercise greater control over the individual than ever before, to make authoritarianism totalitarian.

Can communism change its internal structure and go through a process of liberalization, or is it chained to authoritarianism to such an extent that all communists states must be police states? This question is often asked. Communist and noncommunist Western intellectuals alike have maintained that authoritarianism is only a passing phase, the result of capitalistic and imperialistic pressure. With the consolidation of communist regimes and the weakening of internal opposition and external antagonism, an era of liberty will be introduced and the withering away of the state, foreseen by Marx, will become a reality. In theory most things are possible. On the basis of recent and remote historical evidence, however, this optimistic view of the future of communism seems to be based on a number of misconceptions. These concern such fundamentals as the communist ideology, the nature of collectivism, and the influence of political institutions established by communism.

In relation to the ideology, communists start from the fallacy that property is the only source of differences among human beings, and is therefore the only source of tension and friction. From this fallacy derives their proposition that with the establishment of collectivism the problem of the relationships between groups with different values, aspirations, and interests will no longer arise. All will share the same values, aspirations, and interests. Another fallacy is the postulate that all people occupying the same position in the economic structure have identical views and aspirations. Actually, property is only one of many elements that can lead to differences and antagonisms. Moreover, economic groups (wage and salary earners, operatives, managers, farmers, big and small business, and so forth) behave like all other groups. If there is freedom of expression and of action, they will split whenever they face a problem. Collectivism makes wage earners of all citizens: if they have freedom they will split into majorities, pluralities, minorities. Refusing to face the problem of differences, communists have no other course than to suppress the freedom that brings differences into the open.

Whatever the socioeconomic structure of a state, as soon as there is any freedom, there are divisions. Some citizens want change. Some do not. Any problem facing the community brings varied responses. Democracy, through recognition of the legitimacy of differences, of dissent and of opposition, implies a procedure that enables varied groups to live more or less peacefully together. As the communist mind recognizes neither differentiation nor the legitimacy of deviation and opposition, what is different is either error or evil—if error to be corrected, if evil to be destroyed. If communists were to be tolerant, their tolerance would resemble that of Ottoman Turks who allowed the "infidels" to survive but considered them subhuman. Ideologically, the idea of the liberalization of communism is self-contradictory. Only the weakening of the ideology could lead to liberalization.

With regard to the nature of collectivism, experience shows that discipline and authority are necessary for the proper functioning of economic enterprises. In a capitalist society there are vast numbers of different enterprises. Because of their multiplicity, because of conflicting interests that separate industry, agriculture, trade and credit, as well as employers and employees, management and labor—in other words, because of the division of power characteristic of democratic societies—the enforcement of authority and discipline is limited. In a collectivist society one huge corporation embraces the whole of the economy; its very size requires a complicated and rigid authoritarian and disciplinarian structure; planning cannot be disrupted by independent decisions reached by this or that branch of the economy, by one or another group of producers. Under such conditions, it is difficult to see how the economy can be run except on a basis of total authority and total discipline. And if the economy and state are one, how can this entity act in an authoritarian way in its economic activities and freely in its political activities? If the collectivist state were to be politically free, the slowness, vacillations, dissent, and neutralization of conflicting forces which often characterize democratic procedures, might bring the economy to a standstill. If the efficiency of the economy is to be maintained, democratic procedure must be abolished—as was done in the Soviet Union, in China, and in the so-called People's Democracies. In the 1962–1963 structural reform of the Soviet economy, decentralization of functions was accompanied by centralization of power.

Since the beginning of civilization there have been many collectivist societies. Not a single one has ever known free institutions. Because of the absence of private wealth in the modern collectivist society, whatever the individual wishes to achieve can be realized only through state authorization. No magazine can be printed unless the state provides the newsprint; no organization can have its headquarters unless the state provides the building; no meeting can be held unless the state provides the place. Miracles can happen; but it is wiser to believe in miracles (especially economic and political ones) after they have happened, and not before. Meanwhile, it is well to note that in all communist-controlled states despotism and collectivism have gone hand in hand, and that communists are satisfied with what they have achieved politically in the states they control. They accept what Stalin once wrote: "Repression at home has become superfluous, because with the suppression of exploitation and the disappearance of exploiters, there was no one left to suppress." [1]

Whatever their original intentions, Lenin and his collaborators proceeded to organize Russia on the basis of a totalitarian dictatorship. Dictatorships (usually of a more oligarchic type than the Soviet one) have been established in the other countries in which communists have seized power. Once an institution has been brought into existence, it is hard to modify it, harder still to abolish it. There are very few instances of dictatorships that ended of their own volition. The end usually came as the result of internal conflict or external attack; in the absence of either, dictatorships may last for centuries. If communist thinking included the autonomy of the individual, the control of the citizens over the government, the legitimacy of opposition, there would be a possibility of change. But it was their abhorrence of these very ideas that induced the communists to cut themselves off from what, until then, had been the main stream of socialism. If communists were to put an end to the use of the coercive powers of the state they would no longer be communists, but would be that which, next to the United States, they hate the most: democratic socialists.

The "withering away" of the communist state (that is, the elimination of the means of coercion) is even more out of the question than any major or minor

---

[1] J. Stalin, quoted in *Contemporary Political Science,* Paris: UNESCO, 1950, p. 404.

liberalization of the communist movement, and for the same reason: the inability of communists to cope with the pluralism that results from a relaxation of political controls, except through violence. Lenin solved the problem of the political structure of communist society through the formula of the one-party state. What was supposed to be a temporary solution has become permanent. The communist goal, politically, is a maximum of stability combined with a maximum of centralization. In view of what has been done since 1917 and their goal, communists are likely to improve on the one-party state and make it a straightforward closed oligarchy. Not the party, but the party officials are the ruling oligarchy in communist-controlled states; in the Soviet Union it is comprised not of the 10 million party members but of the relatively few individuals who control the hierarchically organized party.

After seizure of political power, one of the communists' main concerns is the expansion of the economy. Thanks to the concentration of all available capital in the state and the direction of labor by planners with unlimited power, as well as to the rapid formation of new capital, initially obtained by lowering standards of living, successes can be, and have been, remarkable—particularly in fields where large bureaucratic enterprises are most efficient. Successes have been highly publicized. However, they have been no greater than those achieved by free-enterprise economies during corresponding periods of industrial expansion (in Germany, Japan, Sweden, and the United States, for instance, during the four decades preceding World War I). Also, they have cost considerably more both in economic and human terms.

In the decade following Stalin's death, as many free-enterprise countries doubled their national income as did communist countries. In the immediate future, one may assume that in extractive and manufacturing industries the rate of expansion in communist countries is likely to remain high. Standards of living will improve slowly. In terms of long-range developments, however, it is doubtful that energetic leadership and purposeful, unified direction will always be able to offset the damaging effects of bureaucraticism and repression of individual initiative. In collectivism, as in precapitalistic mercantilism, spurts of dynamism depend on energetic political leadership. Without it, collectivism, like mercantilism, tends to fall into a morass of slowness, inefficiency, and waste.

The rate of economic growth in communist states is important when we consider their relations with noncommunist states. It can be considered relatively unimportant with regard to the internal strength of a communist state. Lacking the possibility of making comparisons and unable to apply their critical faculties to an objective analysis of their conditions, citizens of communist states will, after a few years of dictatorship, believe whatever their leaders tell them about the achievements of collectivism and its superiority over all other economic systems.

In the field of intellectual activities, the experience of communism is not likely to differ from that of other despotic societies. "The ascent of humanity . . . may be summarized as a succession of victories of consciousness over blind forces," wrote Trotsky, who had a rationalist's concept of what makes for progress.[2] "Science and the arts can attain full bloom only if there is the fullest freedom of the individual and of society," wrote Khrushchev, correctly.[3] But the freedom

[2] L. Trotsky, *The Russian Revolution*, New York: Doubleday & Company, Inc., 1959, p. 483.

[3] M. Kharlamov and O. Vadeyev, eds., *Face to Face with America, The Story of N. S. Khrushchev's Visit to the USA*, Moscow: Foreign Languages Publishing House, 1960, p. 225.

that makes for intellectual advancement—free inquiry and liberty of expression—is theoretically negated by communist dogmatism and practically negated by communist despotism. "In the pretensions of contemporary communism of being, if not the unique and absolute, but in any case the highest science, are hidden the seeds of its despotism," said the former second most important man in Yugoslav communism.[4] There have been instances of despotisms that allowed sufficient freedom of expression in some fields to promote advancement (in science, in the case of Hellenistic monarchies, in the humanities, in the case of Italian *signori*). Physicists enjoy considerable freedom in countries of the Soviet bloc. But these are exceptions.

The norm of despotic societies is the repression of intellectual activities. As long as there are men whose minds are still in the process of formation in the period preceding the consolidation of despotism—when at least some liberty of thought is tolerated—there may be brilliant intellectual developments. As generations go by, despotism gradually represses creativeness, and intellectual stagnation ensues. In a communist society this is likely to happen more rapidly than in past authoritarian societies because the communist conceptual framework, dialectical materialism, is a particularly narrow one, and means of thought control (censorship and monopoly of education) are considerably more efficient in the twentieth century than they ever were before. So far, communist-controlled societies have shown considerable capacity for imitation, but they are not likely to produce brilliant innovators.

Disillusionment, and the consequent abandoning of

---

[4] M. Djilas, *The New Class*, New York: Frederick A. Praeger, Inc., 1957, p. 2.

communist positions, will probably touch the rising communist generation less than it did the previous one. In communist-controlled countries little is known about the outside world, and that little is greatly distorted. As people react to what they know and as the superiority of communism over all other systems and the evils of "capitalism" (that is, democracy) are taken for granted, the formation of meaningful protest movements against communism becomes less and less probable. Dissatisfaction is therefore unlikely to reach the level of anticommunist agitation. The more than 12 million people who have thus far fled from communist dictatorships and those who attempted to revolt against communism in Russia in 1918–1921, in Eastern Europe in 1953 and 1956, in China in 1959, belonged to groups that were anticommunist before the communists came into power. Outside communist-controlled countries, the majority of those who now join the communist movement have no connection with democracy. Unlike many Westerners who embraced communism in previous decades, they are not prone to disillusionment. The cases of Djilas, Malraux, Roy, Silone, and thousands of others who had genuinely seen in communism the fulfillment of democratic aspirations are not likely to be duplicated by Africans, Asians, and Latin Americans, who are convinced that political totalitarianism, intellectual dogmatism, and bureaucratic collectivism are good per se, not just temporary expedients. Moreover, communist states and communist parties have become better organized to take care of possible dissensions and deviations.

If the weakening of communism through the disillusionment of party members or the dissatisfaction of citizens in communist-controlled countries is unlikely, the same cannot be said of tensions within communist oligarchies. Differences have arisen on questions of principles and policies. There have been personal rivalries. The greater the power, often the fiercer the struggle for it. Also, in a communist state, political power is the best road to wealth. As generations go by, the missionary spirit that at present inspires many communist leaders will be replaced more and more by materialistic considerations. In the European satellite states, agreement is enforced by the Presidium of the CPSU. But in Yugoslavia, in China, in a few smaller states, power is in the hands of communist oligarchies that are autonomous vis-à-vis the Soviet. The falling out of Chinese and Soviet communist leaders, which was once a possibility, has become a reality. Another element of tension in a communist state is the fact that there exists neither political principle nor legal procedure for the transfer of power. Succession will usually be settled on the basis of an agreement among members of the oligarchy. There will be occasions, though, when succession will have to be settled by force, and force may mean anything from a "palace revolution" to a civil war.

The present leaders of the communist states, from Mao to Kadar, are mostly people endowed with strong personalities that were molded in periods of storm and stress. The coming leaders, as is already apparent in the Soviet Union with Brezhnev (1906–   ) and Kozlov (1908–   ), are as fanatical and bigoted as their elders, but their personalities are less impressive. They are the product of a highly bureaucratized society, not of a hard struggle for survival in a competitive world. The qualities leading to communist success in noncommunist states are not the qualities that lead to success within a communist-controlled society, which demands servility, blind obedience, and absolute conformity. However dangerous it is to prophesy, it is not unlikely that, as time goes on, the quality of

leadership in communist-controlled societies will gradually deteriorate. This would lead—in the long run—
to a deterioration of communist institutions.

As to communist prospects outside the countries
they now hold: the advance of communism in the
foreseeable future is unlikely in most advanced democratic nations, but it is probable in the underdeveloped
nations. These are distributed in three main areas of
approximately the same size, but unequal in population and different in cultural background. The most
populous is that of ancient and advanced civilizations,
Buddhist, Hindu, Islamic. It spreads from Indonesia
to Morocco. There, deeply-rooted traditional values
and institutions constitute a major obstacle to the
advancement of communism. On the other hand, several factors favor it: the rapid growth of a restless
intelligentsia which succumbs easily to the appeal of
Marxism-Leninism; the procommunism inherent in the
deeply-felt hatred for everything (real or imaginary)
connected with the West; the excessively close race
between population explosion and economic expansion;
the near-starvation level at which hundreds of millions
live; the impossibility of cooperation between tra-
ditionalists and noncommunist progressive minorities;
the arrogance of the privileged classes. Communists
are hard at work in Indonesia and India, in South
Vietnam and Iran, in Syria and Algeria. In some areas
they have had setbacks; in others, they have made
remarkable progress. The establishment of communist
control over half a dozen nations of this area is within
the realm of short-term possibilities.

The second area is sub-Sahara Africa. Except in
Ethiopia and parts of the Sudan, this area does not
encompass any ancient civilization whose values would
conflict with those of communism. Educated people
are few and, understandably, their main passion is

hatred of Western colonialism—the only political thought they have been aware of during the few decades in which they have been intellectually conscious. Together with Western colonialism, they reject everything which to their minds connotes the West. For people without an intellectual tradition of their own, the simple, sophomoric dogmatism of Marxism-Leninism has a greater appeal than complex Western critical thought. On the other hand, new-found nationalism makes the African intelligentsia—the only element of the population at present participating in political activities—suspicious of all foreigners. In communist plans, gaining control in African states belongs to a more distant future than does the seizure of power in southern and western Asia. (But events rarely develop according to plan: there may be a communist republic in Africa before there is another in southern Asia.) Meanwhile, a main communist concern is the political training of young Africans. Several years are likely to pass before the training gives results in the form of large-scale communist activity in Africa. But quite suddenly, and sooner than many expect, communism may be a major element on the African political scene.

Finally, there is the majority of Latin American states—both the nondemocratic ones and those with shaky democratic institutions. Latin America is of great interest to the communists, not so much for its own sake as for its close relationship with the United States. During four decades of activity, communists have been unable—except for short periods in a few cases—to go beyond the influence exercised over limited circles of the intelligentsia. They tried hard to establish themselves by riding on the tail of movements for which they often had little sympathy: Mexican agrarianism, *Getulismo, Peronismo,* even *Batistismo.* In spite of their efforts they made little head-

way. They have been more fortunate with *Fidelismo,*
but even with the *Fidelistas* communists need to watch
their step. The game communists are playing in the
nondemocratic countries of Latin America is a difficult
one. But to help them there is the precedent of the
Russian revolution, when the powerful revolutionary
force was represented by the agrarian socialists of the
Socialist Revolutionary Party. The Socialist Revolutionaries were unable to organize a democratic republic; they destroyed, and then the Bolsheviki took
over. *Fidelismo,* or some similar manifestation of radical agrarian revolutionarism, could suddenly help
small communist minorities to seize power.

Communism has probably not yet reached the high
mark of its expansion. It is receding in advanced
democracies; but the same factors that once rapidly
made it a primary political force in the nations of
continental Europe are at work elsewhere. The schisms
that may cause temporary setbacks are not likely to
neutralize these factors permanently. There is poverty,
and the consciousness of it. But these are not the
most important elements: different solutions exist for
the problem of poverty, and democracy has done better
than any other system in reducing this problem. The
source of communist strength lies elsewhere: the majority of the fast-growing intelligentsia in the underdeveloped areas of the world reject the critical thinking that makes liberty understandable. They are at
the level of dogmatic thinking where force, now as
in the past, is the solution to problems. Like all ex-
tremisms, communism thrives on dogmatism and
fanaticism: both seem to be on the increase in many
parts of the world.

However tentative and hypothetical, a conclusion
can be drawn from the previous pages. If it is not
the strongest single movement in the world in this
second half of the twentieth century, communism is

certainly one of the strongest. Its strength derived originally from the revulsion in free societies for the conditions of suffering and oppression under which hundreds of millions were living in the Eastern Hemisphere. First liberalism, then democracy had exposed suffering and oppression and brought emancipation in all fields. But communists, and others, were convinced that liberalism and democracy were the source of both suffering and oppression. Today there is more and more evidence that in democracies the suffering caused by poverty already belongs largely to the past, and that oppression, whether of laboring masses or of colonial peoples, is coming to an end. The strength communism derived from the defects of free societies is waning.

In the long run, because of its totalitarian structure, it will be difficult for communism to produce from inner resources the energy needed to maintain fresh life in the movement and in the institutions of communist-controlled states. A process of stagnation is therefore likely to set in, but it is impossible to say how soon this will start happening. If noncommunist states can—and there is no reason why they should not, unless seized by panic—hold their own for another generation or so, they may well be faced at the beginning of the twenty-first century by a communism that has lost much of its present dynamic energy, a communism whose institutions are becoming empty and brittle shells, and whose leaders and followers, instead of being crusaders, have become mere bureaucrats.

The communist leaders have already made a number of serious errors, if by error we mean taking an action that gives different results from those planned. Several, of varying importance, deserve mention. In 1918 Lenin and his friends were convinced that within a few years all Europe would have gone communist;

for five years they engaged in revolutionary tactics
that instead strengthened anticommunist forces. In
1928 Stalin and the Comintern decided that the shortest
cut to the triumph of communism in Europe was to
help the authoritarian right to destroy the main enemy,
democracy. The result was the sudden expansion of
fascism, which proved stronger in the Eastern Hemisphere than either democracy or communism, and
would have destroyed the Soviet Union if the latter
had not been helped by what remained of liberal
democratic states. In 1945 the Soviet Politburo was
certain that an economic crisis would engulf the United
States and therefore decided on a policy of aggressiveness. The result was a strengthening of the anticommunist feeling in the United States and greater resistance
to Soviet expansion.

Since 1948, the top communist leadership has made
several mistakes. Tito was excommunicated on the
assumption that the Yugoslav masses would revolt
against him: they did not. The Korean war was
launched in 1950 on the assumption that the United
States would not fight back: it did fight back. The
violent renewal of aggressiveness by China and the
USSR at the end of 1958 was linked to the conviction
that the American recession would soon turn into a
major crisis: it did not. Faulty planning led to an
economic near-disaster in China in 1960–1961. The
attempt to use Cuba as a military base in 1962, in
order to bring pressure to bear on the United
States, was the result of a wrong Soviet evaluation
of the American nation and the American government.

Through the concourse of unforeseen circumstances,
none of these errors damaged the communist movement permanently. But what has been true in the
past may not necessarily hold true in the future. "The
error of communism lies in its refusal to face the fact

that this is a complex world," [5] wrote a sympathetic critic. Simplification of problems and situations according to rigid theoretical schemes can help when deciding on a course of action, but it can be carried too far.

Whatever the future may hold, the present does not justify complacency where communism is concerned. It stands today as a most successful political movement, less Utopian than it was in its early revolutionary phase. It has built an efficient institutional structure and its dynamism shows no sign of abatement. It enjoys the advantages of skilled and courageous leadership and, in many parts of the world, a wide popular base. It has now become, first and foremost, a machine for the conquest of political power. There was a beautiful dream, and it is still dreamed by many who see reality through the lenses of utopianism. But for those who believe in freedom, the reality of communism is a tragic one. And there is no use deluding oneself that communism will be transformed through an internal process.

Looking at what is and not at what should or might be, at the institutions of the communist states and of communist parties, there is no escaping the conclusion that communism negates the noble attempt made during the last 300 years by nations of Western civilization to make liberty the basis of the social order. This attempt meant evolving institutions through which continuous, peaceful change could take place, replacing arbitrary rule with rule by law and government by force with government by discussion, enabling people and groups pursuing different aims to coexist peacefully. This experiment in freedom is still at a beginning stage. To carry it further communism, and all totalitarianisms, must be opposed.

[5] H. Laski, *Communism*, London: Butterworth & Co. (Publishers) Ltd., 1927, p. 250.

Bibliographical Note

In this bibliographical note are listed a few dozen books of uneven worth, which can help in acquiring greater knowledge and a correct understanding of communism.

The works that follow concern communism as a movement, communist ideology, and the leaders most influential in molding the institutions of communist societies:

Berdiaev, N. A., *The Origin of Russian Communism,* London: Geoffrey Bles, Ltd., 1937. A balanced view of the interaction between communism and the Russian people.

Borkenau, F., *World Communism,* New York: W. W. Norton & Company, Inc., 1939. The best account of communism up to World War II that has appeared in the United States.

Bukharin, N. I., *The ABC of Communism,* Glasgow: Socialist Labour Press, 1921, and *Historical Materialism: A System of Sociology,* New York: International Publishers Co., Inc., 1925. Clear and unsophisticated communist interpretation of Marxism.

Communism in Action, Washington, D.C.: U.S. Government Printing Office, 1946. A concise summary of the general position and the aims of communism, as correct now as when it appeared.

Crossman, R. H. S., (Ed.), *The God that Failed*, New York: Harper & Row, Publishers, 1950. Describes the intellectual crisis of six excommunists and fellow-travelers, reflecting the experience of many liberal-minded Westerners who misunderstood the nature of communism.

Daniels, R. V., *The Nature of Communism*, New York: Random House, Inc., 1962. An exhaustive, typically American view of communism, the result of extensive research and much reflection.

Deutscher, I., *Stalin, A Political Biography*, New York: Oxford University Press, 1949, *The Prophet Armed, Trotsky: 1879–1921*, New York: Oxford University Press, 1954, and *The Prophet Unarmed, Trotsky: 1921–1929*, New York: Oxford University Press, 1959. Valuable biographies if one discounts the emotional involvement of the author.

Djilas, M., *The New Class*, New York: Frederick A. Praeger, Inc., 1957, and *Conversations with Stalin*, New York: Harcount, Brace & World, Inc., 1962. Important attestations on the reality of communism.

Hunt, R. N. C., *The Theory and Practice of Communism*, New York: The Macmillan Company, 1951. Accurately describes Marxist doctrine and its communist application.

Koestler, A., *Darkness at Noon*, New York: The Macmillan Company, 1941, and *The Yogi and the Commissar*, New York: The Macmillan Company, 1945. Among other books by the same author, useful for a correct understanding of communist reasoning.

Lenin, V. I., *Selected Works*, 2 vol., Moscow: Foreign Languages Publishing House, 1950–1952. Contains the essence of the Leninist position; clarity and truthfulness are among the qualities of Lenin as a writer.

Mao, Tse-tung, *China's New Democracy,* New York: New Century Publishers, 1944. A brief statement on the position of the leader of the most populous communist state.

Marx, K., *Selected Works,* 2 vols., New York: International Publishers Co., Inc., 1936–1939. Includes the relevant parts of Marxist ideology adopted by the communists.

Milosz, C., *The Captive Mind,* New York: Alfred A. Knopf, Inc., 1953. A study of communist dogmatism and fanaticism.

Monnerot, J., *The Psychology and Sociology of Communism,* Boston: The Beacon Press, 1953. Provides an insight into the depth of the emotional appeal to which communism owes its strength.

Seton-Watson, H., *From Lenin to Khrushchev: The History of World Communism,* New York: Frederick A. Praeger, Inc., 1960. A popular narrative by a competent British historian, on the development of communism.

Shub, D., *Lenin,* New York: Doubleday & Company, Inc., 1948. A lively, rather superficial biography.

Stalin, J., *Leninism, Selected Writings,* New York: International Publishers Co., Inc., 1942. Contains the essence, not of Leninism, but of Stalinism. All the works by Stalin are worth reading, for a correct understanding of communism.

Tomasic, D. A. *National Communism and Soviet Strategy,* Washington, D.C.: Public Affairs Press, 1957. Mainly a discussion of Titoism; analyzes some of the centrifugal tendencies existing within communism.

Whitney, T. P., (ed.), *The Communist Blueprint for the Future,* New York: E. P. Dutton & Co., Inc., 1962. Contains basic documents concerning the communist position, and a good introduction summarizing the goals of communists everywhere.

Wolfe, B. D., *Three Who Made a Revolution*, New York: The Dial Press, Inc., 1948. A popular account of the lives, aspirations, and activities of Lenin, Trotsky, and Stalin.

Works by more than one author need to be read for correct knowledge of the Russian revolution. Among the many books available are the following:

Carr, E. H., *The Bolshevik Revolution, 1917–1923*, New York: The Macmillan Company, 1951–1953. Should be read keeping in mind that it is based mainly on official documents and therefore contains considerable lacunae.

Chamberlin, W. H., *The Russian Revolution, 1917–1921*, New York: The Macmillan Company, 1952. An exhaustive, definitely anti-Soviet account of the revolution.

Chernov, V., *The Great Russian Revolution*, New Haven, Conn.: Yale University Press, 1936. Describes the events from the viewpoint of a Right Revolutionary Socialist.

Footman, D., *Civil War in Russia*, New York: Frederick A. Praeger, Inc., 1962. Presents through a few major episodes the picture of the political and military conflict of 1918–1921 in Russia, from which communism emerged triumphant.

Kerensky, A., *The Catastrophe*, New York: Appleton-Century-Crofts, 1927. Largely the personal narrative of the man who, in 1917, happened to lead the Russian provisional government.

Lenin, V. I., and J. Stalin, *The Russian Revolution*, New York: International Publishers Co., Inc., 1938. Important from the point of view of communist revolutionary strategy.

Miliukov, P. N., *Russia To-day and To-morrow*, New York: The Macmillan Company, 1922. The sad but basically optimistic account by the main spokesman for Russian pre-1917 liberalism.

Trotsky, L., *The History of the Russian Revolution*, New York: Simon and Schuster, Inc., 1932. The brilliant and, of course, highly partisan narrative of the man whose role was inferior only to that of Lenin.

Among the studies of communism in a regional or national setting are the following:

Alexander, R. J., *Communism in Latin America*, New Brunswick, N.J.: Rutgers University Press, 1957. Describes in detail nearly four decades of communist activities south of the Rio Grande.

Bauer, R. A., A. Inkeles, and C. Kluckhohn, *How the Soviet System Works*, Syracuse, N.Y.: Syracuse University Press, 1956. Contains findings of interviews with Soviet displaced persons.

Borkenau, F., *European Communism*, London: Faber & Faber, Ltd., 1951. Deals with the period when western Europe was the main target of communist pressure.

Brant, C., B. Schwartz, and J. K. Fairbanks, *A Documentary History of Chinese Communism*, Cambridge, Mass.: Harvard University Press, 1952. Contains much valuable material.

Brimmell, J. H., *Communism in South East Asia, A Political Analysis* New York: Oxford University Press, 1959. Deals with the area that replaced western Europe as the main field of communist penetration in the fifties.

Brzezinski, Z., *The Soviet Bloc: Unity and Conflict*, Cambridge, Mass.: Harvard University Press, 1960. Describes developments in eastern Europe after the communist take-over.

Einaudi, M., (ed.), *Communism in Western Europe,* Ithaca, N.Y.: Cornell University Press, 1951. Limited mainly to a discussion of communism in France and Italy.

Fainsod, M., *How Russia is Ruled,* Cambridge, Mass.: Harvard University Press, 1953. A clear, complete exposé of the institutional structure of the Soviet Union.

Freidin, S., *The Forgotten People,* New York: Charles Scribner's Sons, 1962. A lively, deeply felt account of the European nations that came under communist rule during World War II.

Howe, I., and L. Coster, *The American Communist Party, A Critical History (1919–1957),* Boston: The Beacon Press, 1957. The best account of communism in the United States.

Kennedy, M. D., *A Short History of Communism in Asia,* New York: Frederick A. Praeger, Inc., 1957. Deals primarily with the areas of Far Eastern Civilization and with India.

Laqueur, W. Z., *Communism and Nationalism in the Middle East,* New York: Frederick A. Praeger, Inc., 1956. A thoughtful analysis of the potentialities of the communist movement in seven Middle Eastern countries.

Masani, M. R., *The Communist Party in India,* New York: The Macmillan Company, 1954. The most complete account of communism in the Indian subcontinent during the period of monocentrism.

Mu, Fu-sheng, *The Wilting of the Hundred Flowers,* New York: Frederick A. Praeger, Inc., 1962. The book describes what happened to the Chinese intelligentsia under the communists.

Nagy, I., *On Communism,* New York: Frederick A. Praeger, Inc., 1957. Reveals the tragedy of Hungary and of communism elsewhere in 1956.

Niemeyer, G., *Communists in Coalition Governments,* Washington, D.C.: American Enterprise Institute, 1963. A good exposé of what happens when noncommunists try to cooperate with communists.

Ponomaryov, V. N., *et. al., History of the Communist Party of the Soviet Union,* Moscow: Foreign Languages Publishing House, 1960. Gives the official (and everchanging) Soviet view.

Schapiro, L., *The Communist Party of the Soviet Union,* New York: Random House, Inc., 1960. The most complete history of Soviet communism to appear so far.

Schneider, R. M., *Communism in Guatemala, 1944–1954,* New York: Frederick A. Praeger, Inc., 1959. Describes in detail the influence that a small group of determined communists can exercise.

Schwartz, H., *Russia's Soviet Economy,* Englewood, Cliffs, N.J.: Prentice-Hall, Inc., 1954. Describes Soviet economic institutions, their successes and failures.

Seton-Watson, H., *The East-European Revolution,* 3d. ed., New York: Frederick A. Praeger, Inc., 1956. Describes the communist takeover in Eastern Europe, and its results.

Taborski, E., *Communism in Czechoslovakia, 1948–1960,* Princeton, N.J.: Princeton University Presss, 1961. A detailed survey of events in the westernmost (geographically and culturally) Soviet satellite.

Trager, F. N., *Marxism in Southeast Asia,* Stanford, Calif.: Stanford University Press, 1959. A scholarly account of the progress of Marxism, in its various interpretations, in a large and vulnerable area.

Ulam, A. B., *Titoism and the Cominform,* Cambridge, Mass.: Harvard University Press, 1952. The story of the break between Soviet and Yugoslav communism and its immediate impact in eastern Europe.

Zagoria, D. S., *The Sino-Soviet Conflict 1956–1961.* Princeton, N.J.: Princeton University Press, 1962. A sound analysis based on accurate information of the dissension between Soviet and Chinese communists.

Index